DI052972

Janice,

Continue to find your masterpiece
with the nettle of kindness,

With Friendship

Sam

SAVING MANNO

What a Baby Chimp
Taught Me About Making the
World a Better Place

SPENCER SEKYER

PUBLISHED BY SIMON & SCHUSTER

New York London Toronto Sydney New Delhi

SIMON &
SCHUSTER
CANADA

Simon & Schuster Canada
A Division of Simon & Schuster, Inc.
166 King Street East, Suite 300
Toronto, Ontario M5A 1J3

Copyright © 2019 by Spencer Sekyer and Omar Mouallem

Photos are courtesy of the author unless otherwise credited. Reasonable efforts have
been made to identify and contact copyright holders for permission and to give credit.
If additional permission is provided, changes may be made to future printings.

All rights reserved, including the right to reproduce this book
or portions thereof in any form whatsoever. For information
address Simon & Schuster Canada Subsidiary Rights Department,
166 King Street East, Suite 300, Toronto, Ontario, M5A 1J3, Canada.

This Simon & Schuster Canada edition April 2019

The students of the author who appear in *Saving Manno* are
fictionalized characters.

SIMON & SCHUSTER CANADA and colophon are registered
trademarks of Simon & Schuster, Inc.

For information about special discounts for bulk purchases,
please contact Simon & Schuster Special Sales at 1-800-268-3216
or CustomerService@simonandschuster.ca.

Interior design by Lewelin Polanco

Manufactured in the United States of America

10 9 8 7 6 5 4 3 2 1

Library and Archives Canada Cataloguing in Publication

Sekyer, Spencer, author
 Saving Manno : what a baby chimp taught me about making the world a better place
/ Spencer Sekyer.
 Issued in print and electronic formats.
 ISBN 978-1-5011-8374-4 (hardcover).—ISBN 978-1-5011-8375-1 (ebook)
 1. Sekyer, Spencer. 2. Human-animal relationships. 3. Animal rescue—Iraq—Dihōk. 4.
Chimpanzees—Iraq—Dihōk—Biography. 5. Biographies. I. Title.
 QL737.P94S45 2019 599.885092 C2018-905211-2
 C2018-905212-0

ISBN 978-1-5011-8374-4
ISBN 978-1-5011-8375-1 (ebook)

For Anders and Christie.
Your love inspires me to make
this world a better place.

Contents

Foreword

In the fall of 2015 I gave a lecture, organized by the Jane Goodall Institute of Canada, in Edmonton, Alberta—part of my almost nonstop tour around the globe. After my talk, there was a book signing, and, as usual, a long line of people formed, waiting to have a few words, get an autograph, and have a photo taken.

There was one person in that line, however, who had a different agenda—Spencer Sekyer was desperate to tell me about an infant chimpanzee named Manno, who was on display at a zoo in northern Iraq. His keepers were not unkind, Spencer told me, but they had little understanding of Manno's needs. Chimpanzees, like us, are social animals with close family bonds. Manno should have been with his mother and other members of the community. Yet he was the sole chimpanzee in the zoo, and only came out of his tiny cage to be photographed with visitors, dressed in human clothes. It was clearly no life for the infant chimpanzee. Moreover, war raged less than a hundred kilometers away in Mosul where forces were battling the Islamic State.

Spencer had made it his mission to rescue Manno from this inappropriate setting. Of course, Manno could not be returned to the

wild, where he belonged, but he could go to a sanctuary where he could socialize with other orphaned chimpanzees, climb trees, and eat a healthy diet. If only we could get permission from the zoo. And a permit from the proper authorities to enable him to travel back to Africa. And enough money necessary for such a venture. A daunting series of challenges, but I could tell that Spencer was a very determined person.

It was a strange experience, to be signing books in North America and talking to a high school teacher about how to transport an infant chimp from war-torn Iraq to a sanctuary in Africa! Of course I told him I would do all that I could to help. The Jane Goodall Institute (JGI) of Canada put Spencer in touch with Daniel Stiles, project manager for the Project to End Great Ape Slavery.

Eventually, thanks to the efforts of Daniel and many other concerned people, Manno was indeed transported to Sweetwaters Chimpanzee Sanctuary in Kenya, a sanctuary that I had worked to establish. It is situated within the Ol Pejeta Conservancy that encompasses 90,000 acres of savannah habitat. There, Manno was gradually introduced to one of the groups that now considers Sweetwaters home—although a home very different from the tropical forests from which most of the orphans had originated.

Sanctuaries like Sweetwaters are vital in the efforts to end the illegal trade of great apes, who are taken from the wild to be sold as pets or for entertainment in circuses, movies, and advertising. Manno is just one of the many victims of this trade. All were snatched, terrified and traumatized, from the dead or dying bodies of their mothers. Other members of the community often try to intercede, and they too may be killed by the poachers.

Animal trafficking is taking hundreds of great apes from the wild every year, most of them chimpanzees. Once there were up to two million chimpanzees ranging across twenty-five African nations, but due to habitat loss, the bushmeat trade, and poaching there are no more than between 200,500 and 300,000 today, and they have become

locally extinct in four countries. Many of those that remain are living in small isolated groups, cut off from other chimpanzees as a result of the destruction of their forest habitats, with little hope of long-term survival. One of the most urgent conservation measures being tackled today is creating corridors enabling these isolated groups once again to make contact with others and exchange genetic material, thus preventing inbreeding.

The JGI is working with other organizations, communities, and individuals like Spencer to end trafficking. We run two sanctuaries for rescued chimpanzees. Our Tchimpounga Chimpanzee Rehabilitation Center in the Republic of Congo is the largest in Africa. Since its doors opened in 1992, we have protected and cared for more than two hundred chimps, all victims of illegal trade. The other is Chimp Eden in South Africa.

But sanctuaries are not enough to put a stop to the illegal trade in wildlife. To save chimpanzees—or elephants or rhinos or the many iconic species now pushed to the brink of extinction—we must alleviate poverty. People need alternative and sustainable sources of income so that they no longer need to kill wildlife simply to meet basic needs—for food or for money.

All of us have a role to play. Demand for pets, trinkets, and souvenirs fuels the worldwide illegal animal trade through which billions of dollars flow. Trafficking wild animals and their body parts would become increasingly less worthwhile if the demand dropped. This is why JGI and other conservation nongovernmental organizations are launching awareness campaigns in the countries that buy wild animals as pets, for entertainment, for ivory carvings, or in the belief that some body parts—such as rhino horn, pangolin scales, tiger bones, and shark fins—have medicinal value. It is the young people who are helping that give me the most hope. JGI's environmental and humanitarian program for young people from kindergarten through university is now in almost eighty countries. And these young people, along with other similar youth groups, are working to educate their

families, friends, and the general public about the cruelty involved in wildlife trafficking and how it is driving some species towards extinction.

How often I hear, when people are talking about conservation, "Think globally; act locally." But if we think of the trafficking of wildlife around the world, we are overwhelmed by the enormity of the task and tend to give up. Instead, we should tackle a problem that we *can* do something about. By enabling one little chimpanzee to move from a lonely life of servitude to a very different life with a group of his kind, Spencer illustrates that one individual can, indeed, make a difference.

For me, my small part in this story came full circle when, during a recent visit to Sweetwaters, I was introduced to Manno. I was able to throw him an orange through the electric fence that keeps the chimpanzees in their spacious enclosure and keeps predators out. I heard his contented grunts as he consumed the sweet flesh. And I watched as he bounced toward one of his new friends, listened to their breathy laughter as they tickled each other. Manno was at home, and I wished I could have shared these moments with Spencer. Because, if not for Spencer, who was able to persuade many dedicated people to play a role in his rescue, Manno would, almost certainly, still be a prisoner, miserable and alone, in far-off Iraq. Slowly, his spirit would have been broken as he sat with dull blank eyes, staring into space. Would another Spencer have found him and determined to rescue him? There is always hope.

I urge you to read this inspirational story of one ordinary man who did something extraordinary and the mischievous chimpanzee who changed his understanding not only of chimpanzees but also of the other amazing animals with whom we share this world and the importance of saving them before it is too late.

Jane Goodall, PhD, DBE
Founder of the Jane Goodall Institute
and UN Messenger of Peace

SAVING MANNO

Prologue

"The world is a book, and those who do not travel read only one page."

—AUGUSTINE OF HIPPO

The lukewarm drink slipped down my throat, filling my stomach with fire, vaulting up into my nose and making me gag. My watering eyes drip-dropped into the shallow wooden bowl as I lowered it from my mouth, and my tears made ripples in the runny concoction that looked, smelled, and tasted like a tobacco chewer's spit cup. Each sip left my lungs breathless and body ablaze, but I chugged it back until the sandy dredges coated my upper lip. I gave the wooden bowl back to Don Luis, the shaman standing at the edge of my stained mattress clad in a white guayabera with colorful cuffs. He took it to the center of the room, which was lit solely by moonlight filtering through the temple's thatched roof in the depths of the Amazon rainforest.

Don Luis had led me here from my cabin in Selva Madre, a twenty-two-hectare chunk of the Peruvian jungle that resembles the Garden of Eden in daylight. At the hour of my ceremony, however, it might as well have been the dark side of the moon. My headlamp illuminated the treaded paths as I followed him through the compound, across planks layered over creeks and ditches, under the brightest stars I had ever seen, and into the temple, where eight

mattresses lay against the walls. He checked behind each one for snakes and gestured for me to choose one. I picked the mattress nearest a screen door to the outhouse, in case I needed more than a bucket to purge. I settled into a yogi position, studying Don Luis's silhouette as he stood at a table mixing liquids from plastic pop bottles with their labels peeled off. He chanted, lit a thick, hand-rolled cigarette, and blew wisps of smoke in the world's four directions, repeating a prayer after each massive exhale. Finally, he approached me with his outstretched arm to take my pulse with his clammy fingers. "Very good," he said, stretching each vowel forever, before returning with the bowl, blessing it with a blast of smoke, and placing it in my hands.

My stomach gurgled within seconds of swallowing the liquid, but there was no immediate effect. I shifted into a balled-up posture under Don Luis's watchful eye, expecting visions and answers to questions I hadn't yet thought to ask. I'd sojourned alone on this spiritual retreat because I was at a crossroads. A brew of blessings and hardships over the previous months had destabilized me, leaving me pondering my purpose in the world.

After thirty minutes, I wondered if I was in the one percentile of people for whom ayahuasca has no psychotropic effects. Just then, my body went numb and my cheeks felt elastic, as if they might droop into my lap. A wave of dizziness overcame me. *Here it comes,* I thought.

From out of the darkness, Emma, my beloved mutt, shimmied toward me. She hopped onto the mattress and rested on her haunches at the edge of the bed, out of reach. She was mangy and malnourished, her skin almost snaking across her ribs, looking as she did when I found her and her nine puppies in a ditch in Kabul, Afghanistan. *This isn't real,* I reminded myself. *Emma died last month.* I lurched forward to pet her but she disintegrated into pixel-like orbs.

As Emma disappeared, four shadows glided toward me like black stratus clouds turned on their sides. Their paces quickened until they

were almost flying, and I reflexively threw my arms over my face for protection.

I fell onto my back, facing the open ceiling, with my eyelids locked closed. My skin began to sweat, and I saw colorful neurons firing behind my eyelids, threading into patterns resembling textiles in Arab souks. I let the hallucinations flow through me, let my stomach churn, let the dizziness rattle my consciousness. I kept touching my face, reminding myself aloud, "This is still me." All the while, Don Luis switched from singing and whistling an *icaro*, a melodic medicine song, to only whistling it. When I opened my eyes, the faint light on his loose white shirt and spread arms in front of me turned him into a soaring eagle. He and the small fire burning at the end of his cigarette were mesmerizing, and I believed I'd seen the essence of his soul.

The cloud-like entities still loomed over me. I opened my eyes to face them. I heard whispering, and I realized what they were. Who they were. They were my critics. The people who have attacked me for helping the needy abroad instead of "our own," or who have called me a white savior for trying to do good. The voices that have lambasted me for rescuing animals instead of people, or dogs in other countries when we have so many strays at home. They were the critics that have condemned me as a try-hard, a show-off, a hypocrite.

Then, a flash of an old dog-eared snapshot from my family album made me smile. It was me and my brother as small boys, holding dead ducks we'd shot on a family hunting trip. My smile in the temple disappeared, but it stayed forever in the photo. Was that a moment of childhood innocence or did it reveal something inherently evil about man? What was wrong with me that remembering that moment after four decades brought me joy? I sprinted through years of hunting innumerable sentient beings, struggling to come to terms with the pain I'd caused. The swallow I'd thrown rocks at on the fairground where I'd worked one summer. All the coyotes I'd hunted, convinced

I was in service to a greater good. They were probably as smart as the domestic dogs that brought love into my heart and changed my life forever. *Am I a hypocrite for my past deeds, or just an evolving animal?* I thought.

I rolled onto my side. My temple throbbed so viscerally that I could have sworn someone was pushing on my ears. I could almost see the outline of a small face close to mine. Was it my unborn child? The boy—I believed—forming in my wife Christie's womb? Or was I the baby in this scene, experiencing the pressures inside the womb of the world? I rolled onto my back to face the vision. It was my son. A miniaturized me, blond-haired and blue-eyed. But he was not alone. Beside him sat a baby chimpanzee of equal size. It was Manno. My friend stuck in a zoo in Iraq, kilometers from a war zone in Mosul, staring at me with those massive brown globes he has for eyes. He stretched out his long arm and placed his wrinkly dark hand on my son's chubby leg. I saw it now. They were one. Their needs were no different. Their instincts the same. Their right to life, to happiness, equal.

As I lay there, now surrounded by the sounds of the jungle, I reflected on the question I had come to answer: *What is the meaning of life?* It was the question that had started me on this journey, and as I stared at the images of my son and Manno before me, I realized the answer had always been there. The meaning of life is love. Of course it is. Love is really all there is. This newfound awareness was beautiful in its simplicity. We all inherently know it. But to feel it in my core was euphoric.

I felt a renewed sense of purpose. I had a responsibility to love. My wife. My family and friends. Animals. Soon, our baby would add more love to our lives. To be of this world is to live for this world, and the highest expression of that is to give love.

The answers comforted me and turned what had started out as an incredibly uncomfortable experience into a calming exaltation. This is the beauty of ayahuasca: it will show you what you need to know,

what you need to work on, but it's on you to do the required work for any meaningful transformation. In that moment, I realized what I had to do—to give love to the helpless, I had to get Manno to a sanctuary so he could live the life he was entitled to live. I had to change his world, not mine.

1: Lessons from Canada

DECEMBER 2013

Chapter one

"*The man who views the world at fifty the same as he did at twenty has wasted thirty years of his life.*"

—MUHAMMAD ALI

You don't know peace until you've worked in a high school and seen it in the early morning. When the building itself feels at rest, oblivious to the frenzy and haste about to rattle its floors, there are fewer places calmer than between those cinderblock walls.

It was just before Christmas break in 2013, and the snow was coming down hard as I arrived at the school that morning. As I banged my boots together to brush off the snow, the hollow thumping echoed off the bulletins and student-made posters. Eager winners of science fairs and invention competitions had pasted their projects on boards with an abundance of blue thumbtacks that bled out at the edges. The glass trophy case displayed faces full of pride and self-esteem, of that look you get when you realize hard work pays off. I'd been to the top of Mount Kilimanjaro, and the summit was not as quiet as these hallways in the precious hour before the hundreds of beige lockers were whipped open and slammed shut, four hundred of them at once. When the scuffling of my socks on the spotless linoleum was the only sound as I padded to my classroom. I sometimes felt that walking school halls at 8:00 a.m. feels like the International Space Station must at all hours—still and vast, empty but for a few

colleagues in their rooms preparing their work with the calmness of lab chemists.

The northern twilight outside my classroom window had turned a foot of fresh powder sapphire. The only other colors across the diluted blue landscape came from Christmas lights along the eaves of houses across the parking lot. In about thirty minutes, that view would be blocked by dusted cars jammed in a tight box by frustrated parents wondering why they were still driving their teenagers to school. It was the only source of light in the room until I flicked on the four switches and the long fluorescent bulbs spasmed to life.

A female student once quipped that my classroom reminded her of her younger brother's bedroom on account of all the posters that adorned the walls. On one side of the class were mementos from my trip to Hanoi: a poster with North Vietnam's Communist crest and a laminated vintage USSR propaganda poster. On the other side hung framed 8 × 10 quotes from Martin Luther King Jr.'s "I Have a Dream" speech and a bright Afghan rug for a hypnotic splash of color to counter the white cinderblock walls and institutional cream-colored linoleum.

Things got more "colorful" at my desk, where I kept photos from my travels: a snapshot of me in white with a red neckerchief extending a tepid hand to graze a vicious Toro Bravo during the Pamplona bull run—not my proudest moment anymore; a framed picture of the Israeli border wall, taken from the West Bank; and a photo of me—a shock of tight blond hair, holding an AK-47 in Afghan garb. When parents asked about it during parent-teacher meetings, I pointed to the picture beside it, the one of me teaching in a Kabul school for street kids, and their wrinkled foreheads smoothed out.

I wanted to demystify the unknown other worlds with firsthand experience, so with every break we got—in December, March, or those two glorious months of summer—I went where most others wouldn't dare. Places that made me appreciate the true meaning of peace more than those quiet hallways ever could.

Around 8:25 a.m., a small pattering of colleagues' footsteps and light chatter formed into a rumble. The stillness outside filled with tires chomping and skidding through snow. The rumble grew into a deafening stampede, a discordant mix of laughing, squealing, calling, slamming, and running, and soon I had to shout over a cacophony of students still acquainting themselves with this thing called socialization.

I took a deep breath and put my index finger over my lips. "Everybody go *shhhhhhhh . . .*" This was my trick—don't *shush* them, make them *shush* each other. Works (almost) every time.

"Merry Christmas, Happy Winter Solstice," I said after it quieted down. A few of them wished one back. "I bet you're all excited to start your vacation tomorrow, though from the looks of it some of you couldn't wait." Five of the desks stood empty; from my experiences of teaching grades seven to twelve, the absences grow with every grade. No matter what their age, though, everyone gets loopy at this time of the year, even the teachers.

School really is a minisociety. You can't predict your next year until another random assortment of teens squeezes into your room and begins a silent dance. Sometimes we fool ourselves into thinking we live in a vacuum, but our lives can change depending on the sequence of personalities that surround us. Any given combination can boost one pupil's confidence or reinforce another's low self-esteem. Even the coordination of desks is important. A single sightline between two students can create a crush that'll form some of their first feelings of love and heartbreak, or a jealousy that'll reveal personal insecurities they won't understand for years to come. But the dance is usually subtler, filled with tiny power dynamics that allow some to lead and others to follow. All these new social dynamics need time to stabilize, so by Christmas break most of us are eager to break from this society.

"Everybody with their textbooks already out of their bags . . ." I announced with a dramatic pause. "Please put them back."

What's his game? their looks said. But after a reassuring nod, the prepared students packed away their hulking brick of a textbook. I couldn't have taught a typical history lesson that day if I'd wanted to. It was 8:45 a.m., and their legs were already bouncing like the oil derricks pumping around the Alberta countryside.

There's an old teaching adage: "Don't smile until Christmas." Sounds harsh, but there's an inkling of truth to it. Each load of students is a fresh slate of relationships that will carry into the next few years, relationships determined by the first weeks of class. The thinking of many teachers is that it's easier to come in strong and relax over time than to gain control of a classroom after they see you as an ally. The first time I heard this proverb was as a fresh and brash physical education teacher. The colleague who said it to me made it sound as though school was a maximum-security prison— show them your prowess or forever be powerless. Hyperbolic it may be—that December day was the sixty-ninth school day of the semester and I'd probably smiled for as much—it's usually best to loosen up over time instead of on day one. That way, by the time you can connect with them personally, you've already established your leadership.

"Let's take a break from the course," I said. "What I want to know today is, who was not born in Canada?"

Only two hands went up. It wasn't unusual for where I taught. Though the city, Edmonton, was a cosmopolitan capital of many income levels, this suburb, Sherwood Park, was a middle-class, primarily white community created out of good-paying oil refinery jobs in the 1970s. The batch of immigrants in 2013 was Carly, a red-headed girl in plaid from the United States—a fact she'd made known numerous times since school started—and a brown-haired boy in a black sweater and skater shoes sitting in the front of the room.

"Where are you from, Ricardo?" I asked.

"Philippines," he said quietly.

"The Philippines," I repeated louder for everyone to hear. Ricardo's

mom arrived ten years ago as a temporary foreign worker. The oil boom had created a shortage of Albertans willing to work many jobs, so the service industry imported them from abroad—she was one of thousands to arrive from the Philippines. Tagalog was the fastest-growing language in the city, the Filipino community was a growing middle class, and Ricardo's deep brown eyes were a glimpse into this student body's future.

"So, right away, you understand something the rest of us don't—something that, as a Canadian born and raised here, I know I didn't understand for a long time," I said. "Tell us, what is it?"

"How actually cold it is?"

I laughed along with the teens. "Believe it or not, Mr. Santos, even those of us who have been here for a while know it's unnatural to live in these conditions. No, but really, what do you think it is that you learned by coming here from far away?"

"How good we have it here," he said matter-of-factly.

"Yes!" I pointed my finger at each of the five rows of desks, lumping their inhabitants together no matter how different they might feel most of the time. "*How good we have it here.* How good do we have it here, Ricardo?"

"Pretty good."

"Not just pretty good—very good." I pushed the projector power button. As the screen lit up, I asked them, "How many of you would like to win the lottery?" Every hand attached to a head that was paying attention rose. "Congratulations, you've already won it. Just by being here. Here, Sherwood Park, Alberta, Canada. You're wealthier than almost everyone in the world."

A website called the Global Rich List flickered on with two entry fields, one for your country of residence and one for your annual income. "Anyone here have an afterschool job?" I asked.

The minimum age for employment in Alberta was twelve. *Twelve!* Still, it was rare for more than a couple of hands to go up, even in a high school. Only Logan, a boy in a black T-shirt, volunteered.

"Where do you work?" I asked.

"McDonald's!" interrupted another boy with a snort.

I *shhh'd* him and asked Logan a second time. He mumbled Mc-Donald's. "Good for you, buddy. Now, do you mind me asking how much you make per hour at McDonald's?"

"Ten-fifty," he said.

"Nice, man," I said, nodding and imagining being lucky enough to make that wage myself at his age in 1983. "So, $10.50, part-time, let's say, what? Fifteen hours per week?" I wrote his hourly wage and "× 15" in dry-erase marker on the whiteboard, humming to myself as I crunched the numbers. "Help me out, guys."

"$157.50," Carly offered, and together, she and I multiplied that by fifty-two weeks, for a grand total of $8,190. I punched the numbers into the keyboard, hit enter, and the screen displayed a stack of one hundred human silhouettes. A flash of gray darkened them from the bottom, snaking from left to right, climbing to the top of the graphic until only the first twenty were unshaded.

"Logan, you are in the top twentieth percentile. Do you know what that means?" His look said, *No.* "It means you, on your own and with no other help, are wealthier than four out of five people on this planet."

"Or the . . ." Logan struggled to count the much bigger number beside the percentage on the screen. "One billionth? Two-hundred—"

Carly interrupted again. "1,239,775,074th richest person by income." She took a long breath. "Is that true?"

"Close your eyes for a minute. Now imagine that the world is a village of one hundred people."

"Can I be president?" asked a deep voice I knew to be Jonathan.

"How about village idiot?" snipped Carly.

"Carly," her budding nemesis Vanessa snapped, "how about you be—"

"Let's not right now, please." I populated the tiny world now existing in their imaginations. "If there were only one hundred

people in your village, half of you would still be male, half of you female. Only fourteen of you would be from North or South America. Most of you would be from Asia. Only five of you would speak English. Twenty-three of you would pray at a mosque. Fourteen of you would be illiterate. Twenty-two of you wouldn't have a safe shelter. Eleven of you would be malnourished. Nine of you wouldn't have access to clean water. One of you would die of starvation today."

I let the rare silence linger. "Now, does that sound like any place you've been?" The silence thickened. "And yet, that's our world. Luckily, one hundred percent of us in this room have safe drinking water. One hundred percent of us have a roof over our heads. One hundred percent of us have eaten a meal in the last twenty-four hours." I added with caution: "Hopefully. Now open your eyes."

On the screen behind me, there was a wide shot of a schoolyard playground with African kids running in the dirt, kicking soccer balls, and climbing rusted poles. "Anyone notice anything about this picture?"

"No shoes," said Ricardo.

"Shoes, to them, are flip-flops, and they take them off to play because those things on our feet are, to them, luxuries."

"Where is that?" Ricardo asked.

"It's Sierra Leone," I replied. "A country in West Africa that had a brutal civil war that started in 1991 and only ended around the year you were born."

"Did you take it?" Carly asked.

"I did. I went there to teach at a summer school five years ago. Back then, it was considered the second least livable place on Earth."

"Why did you go?"

"Because it was considered the second least livable place on Earth," I repeated with a smile. "I wanted more perspective. Is anyone getting on a plane for the holidays?" A few were. Jonathan was going to Cancun with his parents. Another student to Vancouver. A few would see

grandparents out of province, and Carly was going back home to Salt Lake City. "That's awesome. All travel is good. Anything that expands your world, even if it's by a few hundred miles, is great. And the earlier you can start, the better."

"How old were you when you started?" asked Vanessa. I dared the class to guess.

"I don't know, like, eighty?" asked Jonathan. I flashed a mock unimpressed look and then he tried for real. "I'm guessing twenty." I shook my head, raising a thumb to say higher. Another student guessed twenty-five, another thirty-five. My thumb climbed higher in the air. Vanessa guessed forty.

"Close," I said. "Forty-one. That's how old I was when I started really seeing the world, just five years ago. Do any of you have parents under forty-one?" Many did. Too many. I grimaced and covered my eyes. "Ahh, it burns, it burns!" When I peeled my hands off, I saw that I had everyone's attention. No gazing at the clock, no texting, no sketching in their textbooks. A captive room. "In fact, except for traveling around Canada and a few trips to Mexico and the States, I'd spent most of my life within Alberta and British Columbia."

"You're not from Sherwood Park?" asked Carly.

"I'm from a place much smaller, believe it or not. I'm from a town called Dawson Creek."

"Like the show?"

No, nothing like the show. My childhood home was a bungalow in northeastern British Columbia. Our house overlooked a ravine and had no resemblance to the fictitious community at the heart of the 1990s teen drama. The real Dawson Creek was a tough farming, logging, and coal-mining town, and like many small Canadian towns of that era, it could be rough.

Most people in Dawson Creek were friendly, willing to push your

truck out of the snowbank before you even needed to ask for help. But anything you did, good or bad, would be known by almost everyone in town (including my parents) before day's end. On fishing trips, my dad, Gary—a firefighter—would tell me and my older brother, Dean, that when it came to character, reputation and hard work were everything. "Earn what you have, don't expect handouts from anyone, and always be honest."

I got along with most people and I really liked to laugh and have a good time squeezing the most out of each experience. But I was also a product of my town's pugilistic nature, which you could see in my slightly crooked nose that I'd smashed on the ice or the dip on my right hand where my ring finger knuckle should have been, remnants of one of many bar dustups. Long before becoming a social studies teacher, you could say I had no business teaching anyone about civil society.

Growing up at the tail end of the Vietnam War, I absorbed most world affairs from what was on the one TV channel we had or from fiddling around with my grandfather Papa Nelson's mementos from his service in the Second World War. I spent many afternoons sitting at the kitchen table sketching army tanks, choppers, and imaginary battles. As I filled the pages, my mind would drift to dreams of playing pro sports, the rapturous spectators chanting my last name: "See-kerr, See-kerr . . ." By the time I'd snapped out of it, my cartoon soldier's gun would look an awful lot like a hockey stick or his helmet like that of a football player. The only images in my childhood head more vivid than the ones of war in the jungle were the ones of New York Islanders defenseman Denis Potvin kissing the Stanley Cup or Warren Beatty suiting up for the Los Angeles Rams in the 1978 movie *Heaven Can Wait*. A poster of the movie—my favorite as a kid—adorned my wall beside pictures of Potvin, staring at me from between his clumps of shaggy sideburns, his gaze daring me to dream big. Submerged in this fantasy, I made secret bets with myself as I played in the yard. *If you walk along the*

edge of the fence without falling, you'll make the big leagues one day, I'd tell myself.

That athletic spirit was more than just psychological. It was cultural. Canadian kids of my era were practically groomed for athletics. In the 1970s, right around the time of the Montreal Olympics, the government launched a program called ParticipACTION. The jingle—"Don't just think about it . . . DO IT! DO IT! DO IT!"— was everywhere, and so was the propaganda, including in public school.

Every kid between grades three and eight had to take a yearly fitness test, a series of challenges that determined whether they earned a bronze, silver, gold, or, for a select few, the coveted Award of Excellence certificate. I worked hard to do well amongst the other ten-year-olds when it came to push-ups, sit-ups, or flexed-arm hang, and I was often amongst the top runners. But my standing long jump distances weren't even close to the standards needed for an Award of Excellence. I struggled to launch myself farther than a few feet. But my mom, Irene, knew how much earning the Award of Excellence meant to me. So, every day before supper, she took me through the ravine and bushes behind our bungalow and into an empty school field where nobody could see us practice. I see now how my mom went out of her way, without a word spoken between us, to help me reach my goal. Though her sports career was limited to her bowling league, she did her best to teach me how to gain "explosiveness," as she described it, propelling my body forward until my footprints in the dirt were nearly two meters from the jump line. With her help, I earned the Award of Excellence not just that year, but every year I competed. Holding the certificate in my hands for the first time, I realized that if I put in the effort and had the right people to help me along the way, there was nothing I couldn't do.

My parents also tried to prepare me for the real world with their healthy pragmatism. But they couldn't tame my aspirations. If I wasn't

going to play in the NHL, it was the NFL, and if not the NFL, then at least the Canadian Football League. A steadier career like teacher or firefighter wasn't on my mind.

What started as a fantasy felt more like the future with every bigger size of hockey and football jersey that I pulled on. I had one pretty good season as a hockey player when I was nine or ten, until I had to compete with the older boys. Suddenly, the guys around me were playing at a different level. I still worked my hardest, but I struggled to keep up.

A few years later, when I started playing junior hockey as a teenager, I found my place on the roster by squeezing into the one role where I'd win the approval of my teammates and coaches: enforcer. All it would take was a tap on the shoulder from the coach or maybe he'd give me a number, but it was usually obvious what I had to do and to whom I had to do it. I'd hop over the boards, glide toward my target, and tail him around the rink. "C'mon, let's go," I'd taunt my counterpart, sticking to him like a shadow while he chased the puck, draining his patience with each jostle and slash. "C'mon, tough guy. Are your gloves glued on?"

Inevitably, I'd get to him, and then it was on. I had ten seconds, twenty tops, before the refs pulled us apart—just enough time to whip up the crowd and my teammates. Then it was over. I would head to the dressing room, using my last seconds of ice time in the game to wipe my face with my hand and check for blood.

Long before I realized the long-term effects of brawling—the limited short-term memory and frustration of constant forgetfulness that plague me today—I enjoyed it. Loved it, even. I'd get sick with anxiety on game day, knowing I would not sleep that night without a new wound or two. But I relished the adrenaline of winding up my opponents, the roar of the crowd, the euphoria of my teammates' adulation on my way to the dressing room after I'd done my part. I even had a fondness for the starburst that came with a hit, a painless flash that I wouldn't feel until the adrenaline wore off. The downside? If I

lost in our barn, everyone in school saw it, and I'd have to face hundreds of witnesses to my defeat the next day.

I wasn't good enough to advance beyond the junior hockey league that overlapped the borders of northern Alberta and northern British Columbia. Luckily, when I was sixteen, Dawson Creek started its first football team, a group of raw, enthusiastic small-town and farm boys who signed up to relieve excess aggression. At first, there were hardly any spectators at our games, let alone bleachers for them to sit on. The field was a defunct outdoor speed-skating rink with field-goal uprights three feet from perpendicular. The team name—the Penguins—didn't seem to match our hard edges, but given that practice sometimes entailed us braving −30°C weather and sweeping a foot of snow off the grass with curling brooms, the Antarctic bird was appropriate.

Our coach, Brian Thornton, who was also my math teacher, probably doubted most of us would bother graduating, let alone go to college. But after I'd played a few months as both a defensive lineman and fullback, he said to me, "Spence, keep this up and you could go pro." Mr. Thornton made me a captain, and I helped lead our rugged team to the Peace Bowl against the Warriors—a school and team twice our size that was the favorite to win.

The game took place in Dawson Creek on a brutally cold November day. We were sliding across the frozen turf, struggling for balance. But while there wasn't good footing, there was great hitting. We won the game with a landslide victory. The team chose me as its defensive MVP, and the league selected me for its all-star team. Not long after, I was invited to an exclusive training camp in Vancouver with the province's best high school players. My hockey career might have been on the downswing, but suddenly my future in football seemed a little brighter.

I wanted to become Dawson Creek's hometown sports hero. But two letters brought me back to reality.

The first arrived in spring 1986. The University of Alberta invited

me to try out for their varsity football team in Edmonton—the so-called City of Champions and home to Wayne Gretzky, two Stanley Cups, and five consecutive Grey Cup championships courtesy of the CFL's Edmonton Eskimos. It was, for a sports-crazed, small-town Canuck like me, as good as it got.

I made the team, but it wasn't an easy ride. The first time I saw one of my new teammates was in the gym, where he was bench pressing four plates a side—about 405 pounds, and almost twice what I could at the time. The second time I saw him was when I lined up against him in a hitting drill. The coach blew his whistle, and the next thing I knew, I was struggling to peel my back off the field. The impact warped my face mask, and I had to hobble to the lockers after practice.

I wasn't physically ready to play until my third year, and by then, my confidence was eviscerated. I became the player whose only field time was giving postgame slaps on the back. I still hoped it would all turn around, and I wouldn't let go of my dreams of becoming a professional athlete. I did whatever my coaches asked and spent warm-ups diving for balls, just so I could say I'd expended some physical energy on game days.

In my fourth year in Edmonton, the second letter arrived. It was from the Hamilton Tiger-Cats, a CFL team in Ontario, inviting me to their open tryouts. I was elated, but the excitement was short-lived. It was a form letter. I soon realized that everyone in our locker room had received one. To the CFL, all my training and experience was worth only the cost of a postage stamp.

It crushed me, but it didn't surprise me. On my visits back to Dawson Creek, old friends asked when they would see me on the Sports Network. Since disappearing into a puff of smoke wasn't physically possible, I'd tell them about the Tiger-Cats letter, leaving out a few key details. I told the town's sportswriter the same thing, but the reporter, a man who'd gushed about my "excellent talent" in the town paper when I set off for university, saw right through it.

"That's too bad," he said. "I really thought you were going to be something."

My entire sense of self was invested in being an athlete, and now it was crumbling.

That wasn't the only shock to my system, though. Back then, Edmonton was a spread-out, conservative, blue-collar city, but it was still more diverse and compact than any place I'd ever seen. And like most big cities, there was a wider gap between most individuals' values, requiring a wider embrace of the different classes and cultures. I learned that some of the values of my childhood didn't always translate.

I was on a restaurant patio one evening with a friend visiting from Dawson Creek, when someone leaned over the fence to ask us for money. "I already pay you through my taxes," I said, smugly. My buddy and I had a great laugh at the time. Looking back now, I'm ashamed at how gleefully I humiliated that man and how shamefully I acted. There were so many complexities that might have pushed that man to beg, and I had been ignorant of them all. More than that, though, until that point I had been unwilling to learn about them.

One summer, when I was back in Dawson Creek between semesters, I woke up early one morning during a thunderstorm. I stayed up to watch the lightning. While admiring what my dad called "nature's fireworks," I noticed someone was stealing my bike. I bolted outside, chased the guy down, and managed to get my bike back. Later that summer, the local mill foreman told me they'd hired some new workers. I looked at the new group walking in, and there was the same guy I had caught trying to steal my bike; he was just trying to get by like the rest of us. We never talked about it, but if I could go back I would apologize to him. He shouldn't have tried to take my bike, but the retribution I'd delivered far outweighed the infraction.

After four years in Edmonton, I realized there was something

beautiful about having hundreds of thousands of different people around me, challenging my views in ways that weight rooms and hitting drills never would. When the form letter arrived from the Tiger-Cats, I briefly considered flying out there—maybe I was that diamond in the rough?—or trying out for a minor professional hockey team. But it was time to make new goals. I quit the varsity football team and called my parents.

"Dad," I said. "I think I'm going to finish my education degree. I'm going to try to be a teacher."

"Absolutely, Spencer," he said. "It's time to grow up and get a job."

My mom agreed. "I'm so happy you're moving on with your life."

An education degree, I hoped, would open endless possibilities. Already, my head filled with questions about my future: Where would I live? What subject would I teach? What style of teacher would I be? I was leaving behind the version of me who had identified so closely with being an athlete, and another version of me was beginning to sprout. It was exciting and heartbreaking at once.

We spent the rest of class hearing stories from different students about their foreign experiences, however much or little they'd traveled. Some insights were profound, like Ricardo explaining how most of his friends back home lived in single-parent households because there was often one parent working in another country.

Other insights were mundane, like one student's observation that milk in Ontario can come in a bag. But every bit of the conversation helped feed their curiosity, which I could only hope would lead them to see the world outside of a screen. "Any chance you get to travel," I said, "if you can afford it, I hope you'll buy the ticket."

With fifteen minutes before the end of the period, I asked them to open their notebooks to an empty page. The holidays weren't always an easy time for everyone, so each year, I tried to give my students something that would make them feel good about themselves. "Write

the name of the person sitting in front of you at the top of the page," I instructed. "Below it, I want you to write one positive thing about them—"

The groaning of a few cynics interrupted me.

"Come on, you've known each other long enough now that you can all think of at least one positive thing. Just write it down—no 'buts,' because 'but' cancels out the thing before it. You can write, 'Carly has great style,'" I said, looking at Vanessa. "That someone is generous," I said, making eye contact with Carly. "Is funny, has great teeth, whatever. But if you can get more specific, it will have more meaning. Thirty seconds, then pass the paper behind you and write something nice about the next person named on the page you get." I asked Ricardo in the front right corner to start mine, and told Jonathan in the desk farthest from mine that I'd start his.

"Better not be something mean, Mr. Sekyer," he said.

"I'll do my best," I said, smiling and writing his name at the top of a blank sheet and "Jonathan has strong self-confidence" below it.

"All right, thirty seconds . . . go!" They raced to fill the pages with kindness, the scratching of pens and erasers undoing what might come across as too sincere or infatuated. "Switch!" I blurted after every interval. Papers whooshed over their shoulders and slid onto another desk.

When the exercise was done, the quiet fawning began—and the bell rang. The room exploded with sliding chairs and rustling paper as friends shared their page of niceties with one another.

"Wait, Mr. Sekyer!" called Carly, loud enough for everyone to hear and some to stop. "You didn't say if you're going anywhere for the holidays."

"You didn't ask."

"Are you?"

"I am," I said, making my way toward a laminated world map beside the door, dotted with three dozen blue dots, one for each country I'd visited. I pressed my finger against a little mitten-shaped

country in the Middle East. "Here." Carly, Vanessa, Jonathan, Ricardo, and Logan gathered around me, squinting and leaning over my arm to read the four letters above my fingernail. All at once, it clicked in and the students, in a medley of bewildered voices, read it aloud: "*Iraq?*"

Chapter two

"Life is either a daring adventure or nothing at all."

—HELEN KELLER, *THE OPEN DOOR*

In the middle of its descent, our plane abruptly pulled up, waking me with a sudden jolt. The seat-belt signs were already on but the cabin crew flashed them off and on again. I buckled in and peered outside at a runway coming into view. A black blur appeared to be running across the dotted white line just before our wheels touched down. After the passengers applauded a safe landing, as they're known to do in the Middle East, the Royal Jordanian captain made an announcement over the speaker in Arabic. I recognized the first part of his sentence—he welcomed us to Erbil, the capital of Iraqi Kurdistan—but not the second part. In English, he explained: "Apologies, passengers, for that little bump. There was an animal on the runway, so we had to pull up and delay the landing until it was safe." I'd come to the right place.

Two years before, in 2011, a woman in Afghanistan told me about KOARP, the Kurdistan Organization for Animal Rights Protection, a small-scale organization rescuing stray cats and dogs in Iraqi Kurdistan. She suggested I volunteer with them.

After the Arab Spring in 2010, Northern Iraq, unlike the rest of the country—and increasingly the surrounding Middle East—remained stable. That was in large part because of the self-governing Kurdish

Regional Government, a separate parliament born out of the Gulf War. The Kurds are the world's largest ethnic group without a nation, and Iraq's eight million are a sliver of the "real Kurdistan" spread across five countries. After the 2003 invasion of Iraq, their powerful Peshmerga army aided the United States in toppling Saddam Hussein, and in return, they gained more autonomy that allowed them to thrive on lucrative oil reserves and a strong army.

That's not to say Kurdistan hasn't suffered in the turmoil. *Peshmerga* roughly translates to "one who faces death," and many men and women—a curious feature of this Middle Eastern military—have paid with their lives to fight hostile forces on every side of its border, in Iraq, Iran, Turkey, and Syria. Still, attacks in Kurdistan had been rare over the years, a fact I tried to take comfort in.

I threw a faded canvas backpack over my shoulder and dragged a carry-on through the narrow plane aisle into a tunnel crowded with dozens of men in simple blazers and a few modestly dressed women with loose hijabs concealing everything but their bangs. The crowd dispersed into a mostly empty airport, the wheels of their luggage rolling over the three-year-old glossy gray tiles to the two passport control lines. Half of the passengers were citizens, half were NGO workers and financial types. I admired the vaulted ceilings and glistening beams as I waited. The building was bright and polished, but the slots on the big flight screen were mostly empty. Air traffic controllers outside fiddled with their phones in the cement wasteland.

I was called up and my passport was stamped with hardly a question, a favor the olive-skinned Jordanian in front of me did not get. As I entered the baggage-claim area, my last piece of luggage—a bulging duffel bag—rolled off the conveyor belt. Before I'd left, I'd stuffed the bag with all the clothes I had stopped wearing, planning to deliver it to a refugee camp in Kurdistan. It was my tradition to give away tired possessions on these trips, and the only painful part of it was the reminder it served of my own greed. *Seventy-five-dollar boardshorts, what was I thinking?* I could send a child in Sierra Leone to school for

a year for that. I knew that, and yet I was still susceptible to wasteful, selfish spending. I tried to school my students on the glut of Western capitalism, but I often needed a reminder myself.

The first time I'd donated clothes to a camp, I'd unzipped the bag and started handing out items of clothes, but within a minute, there was a crowd of a couple hundred people arguing over who got what. Children were crying because someone had snatched something right out of their hands. Others were fighting over what was, to me, a worthless piece of clothing, wrestling as though their very existence depended upon it. My bag was empty in under five minutes and only a couple dozen people had something in their hands. Worse, I then had to explain to people asking me "What? Not for me?" that I had nothing left to give them.

I shook my head thinking about it as I made my way through the airport. *Give and release, and give wisely, not because it feels good, but because it is good.* I grabbed my duffel bag and stepped out into the desert, determined to do better this time.

The best lessons I've learned in life all started with hopping on a plane, but none of them would have been learned were it not for my time at the front of a social studies classroom, a setting that almost never happened.

After I graduated from university, I was lucky enough to get a job teaching physical education just outside Edmonton. Much as I was grateful to have a full-time job right out of university—and one in the same city I'd studied in, no less—I started off hesitantly. I wanted to be not just a teacher, but a cool teacher, a really great teacher like many of the ones I was lucky enough to have growing up. But at twenty-five, I was basically a kid myself, in charge of high school students not much younger than me. Afraid that I'd never earn the students' respect, I went in like a drill sergeant, particularly with the junior high students. I demanded good behavior from students,

sometimes sentencing students who arrived late to squat against the wall—sixty seconds for every minute they were late, another thirty seconds added if they rose or lowered their legs past that excruciating ninety-degree squat angle.

Don't smile until Christmas? "Sergeant Sekyer"—yes, that's what some kids called me—didn't smile until Easter.

In my mind, I was doing these kids a service by being tough on them. The way I was raised, I was considered late if I wasn't half an hour early for events, curfews, and even social visits. And I couldn't remember ever questioning a coach or teacher for having to run laps for poor effort or behavior. My junior hockey coach made us skate lines in the outdoor rink for an hour after one particularly heinous blowout. I thought of it as character building.

Not everyone shared my outlook, though, and those early years of teaching were lonely. I spent my mornings and days at the school, teaching or coaching, and in the evenings, while other teachers socialized or had dinner with their families, I headed to one part-time job or another. Getting to school at 7:00 a.m., returning home at 7:00 p.m., and spending the last remaining hours before bed writing lesson plans and drafting quizzes. I saw my countless hours spent coaching sport teams stretching indefinitely into the future with little to no variety. I kept looking for a bigger purpose. Something had to change.

Then, one May afternoon in 1998, our principal called me into his office.

"Spencer, we have to make some staffing changes next year," he said, his white shirt and navy tie contrasting with my gray workout gear. "Starting in September, you'll be teaching social studies in room 125."

He pushed over a piece of paper with my teaching schedule the following year printed on it.

I studied the page for a moment. "I'm confused," I said.

"I can see that." He cleared his throat. "I'm afraid this is the only position we have available for you next year. You can take some time to consider your options."

Until that point, I'd only ever taught a single social studies class. I had liked the course material, but I didn't know it well. To that point, I had defined much of my life in physical terms—I'd become so comfortable as a gym teacher. What could I offer as a social studies teacher? This would be more than a career shift—I'd have to step outside my comfort zone and completely rethink how I taught.

I looked at the schedule in my hand again, and I realized there was only one answer. I extended my arm for a handshake.

"I can't wait," I said to the principal.

Sergeant Sekyer was going to need some khakis and dress shirts, not to mention a further education on the world's cultures, economies, and conflicts.

That was a learning curve, to say the least. The first time I taught the Brazil unit, I kept going on about how Brazilians spoke Spanish. Finally, a student raised his hand and said, "Mr. Sekyer, it says here in the text that Brazilians speak Portuguese."

I felt my face go red, embarrassed that I'd made such a huge mistake in front of thirty kids. "It's the same thing," I said, digging my hole even deeper.

As I taught the class, I realized how much I still had to learn about the world. In the process of opening the students' minds to the world, my own mind was stimulated. Slowly but surely, the size of my world grew. I began to understand that things I took for granted growing up—a stable home life, loving parents, friendly classmates—weren't reflective of everyone's reality.

One bright and sunny gorgeous Tuesday morning at the beginning of my fourth year of teaching social studies, I heard something on the radio at home about a plane crashing into New York's World Trade Center. Thinking that a small Cessna or something similar must have inadvertently clipped the building in the fog, I didn't give the news much more thought until I walked through the double doors.

"Mr. Sekyer! Mr. Sekyer!" the kids yelled as they ran toward me,

bombarding me with questions before the large, thick metal doors had time to close behind me.

"Both World Trade towers have fallen down!" a student breathlessly announced with the urgency of being the first to share this news and devastation.

They explained the details to me—two planes, the Twin Towers— as we walked to my classroom, the throng of students clamoring for answers the whole way. I thought back to a man I'd met on a vacation years before who worked at the World Trade Center as a security guard. *Was he still alive?* I wondered.

When we finally got to my classroom, I turned to the students in front of me, who all quieted down.

"What happened today is going to change your lives forever," I said.

What I should have said was that it was going to change *our* lives forever. It certainly did change mine. Social studies suddenly became the most important class for an entire generation.

I scanned the arrivals terminal and eventually wandered outside, looking for a face I knew only from Facebook. From what I could tell, KOARP's director, Dr. Sulaiman Tameer, should be about my age with gray hair, a paper-thin mustache, and a friendly crinkle to his eyes. He'd told me he would welcome me at the airport, but I saw neither him nor a piece of paper with my name on it. It might have been concerning if it weren't so typical for the way I traveled, which was usually as the guest of an NGO. Traveling with an NGO let me give back to the communities I wanted to discover, and it allowed me to immerse myself in local communities so I could experience a place more authentically. But it could also be a dice roll, leaving me in scenarios like this, where the first and seemingly simplest task went sideways.

Before using my phone for an exorbitantly expensive phone call, I stepped outside to see if Sulaiman was parked with the taxis.

A slight brown haze obscured the otherwise cloudless, crystal clear blue sky, and the midafternoon breeze whirled up red dirt and dusted it across the sky. The temperate winter weather had arrivals drawing jackets from their bags, but for me 9°C was practically tropical. Three bearded men draped in long, flowing white linen robes, sheiks maybe, exited the sliding doors with as many suited men dragging full-size suitcases on the tail of their robes. The men in robes stopped before an Escalade, made an inaudible request, and the assistants started falling over themselves to fulfill it, greeting them with a series of traditional kisses on each cheek. The SUV was soon accompanied by two more identical models. The sheiks swept by me, each to his own car, and drove toward the downtown skyscrapers ten kilometers across a wide-open freeway. That's when the familiar panic set in—I'd flown halfway around the world to a foreign country, where I knew no one and no one knew me. *Where is my host? Is he who he says he is? Have I been duped?* The answers to these questions racing through my head got increasingly wild with every passing minute.

Finally, I pulled out my phone and called Sulaiman. He answered before the second ring. "Mr. Spencer?!" His tone startled me somewhat, but I'd soon learn there was a short burst of energy to everything he said.

"Sulaiman?"

"*Yez.*"

"Where are you, man?"

"I'm here waiting."

I looked around. Nope, just taxi drivers, who'd long given up on me, taking long drags of their pencil-thin cigarettes. "Where?"

Sulaiman told me where he was waiting, and from the sound of it, he was at the departures terminal, a different complex altogether and five hundred meters away. When I finally got there, a man waved me down from inside of a low-slung white Toyota pickup decorated with a sort of brown tribal decal across its dusty sides. Sulaiman got out and crammed my luggage into the backseat, amongst a tangle of dog leashes

and veterinary bags. Pamphlets with Kurdish on their covers and science journals were spread across the carpet. It reeked of stale cigarettes.

Sulaiman was stout and potbellied, dressed in a checkered shirt neatly tucked into slacks and a tweed sport coat—what seemed to be the contemporary Kurdish man's uniform. He briskly shook my hand, asked how my flight was, and offered me a cigarette after I settled into the passenger seat. "I don't smoke," I said. He shrugged, like, *suit yourself*, and lit one up for himself.

Erbil is one of the world's oldest cities, inhabited for seven thousand years. But for Sulaiman and me, Erbil was a pit stop. We were heading to Duhok, a smaller northern city near an intersection of the Turkish, Syrian, and Iraqi borders, below the mountains that had served as a refuge for Kurds when Saddam Hussein tried to eradicate them in the early 1990s. "You seriously drove four hours to pick me up?" I asked. "Sorry, Sulaiman, I could have just taken a bus."

"*Yez*, but the bus goes through Mosul," he said. He spoke in starts and stops, with hard commas that I could hear. "It's two-hour drive, *yez*, so it's faster, but Mosul is not good now."

Sulaiman had other speaking quirks. He repeated "*yez, yez, yez*" in the middle of my questions about animal care and the law, and rarely let me finish asking a question before he jumped in with "I will tell you," and then proceeded to tell me in a manner so specific yet frantic that I was left light-headed.

"Are there dog culls in—"

"I will tell you, we have—*yez*, unfortunately, we have—the Stray Dogs Campaign Kill Control Law 48, published in 1971, republished in 1986. What is the difference? I tell you." He sounded off, explaining something to do with a glut of police officers following the end of the war with Iran, then took a long, wet snort as if reloading his verbiage. "For example, in 2010, in forty days in Baghdad, big campaign, they killed 31,440 dogs. In forty days!"

"Did they poison the dogs"—"*yez*"—"or shoot them"—"*yez*"—"or"—

"*Yez.* For example, in 2011, in thirty days, they kill—in Mosul only—they kill 276,525."

"Why?"

"Just to clean the streets."

"Were the dogs hurting people?"

"No, I will give you another example," he said, and then told me of the 6,000 dogs Iraqi Kurdish police killed last year because two people had died of rabies.

As he talked, Sulaiman sped along the road and veered over the center line, even when the highway squeezed to one lane in each direction. He only steered into his own lane when there was oncoming traffic, a practice I might have questioned were it not for all the other cars doing the same thing. He slowed only for donkeys, even when they were far from the road, often just so he could snap a picture of them. Sulaiman got worked up about every creature in view as if he was seeing the species for the first time. He loved animals to his core and wasn't afraid to show it. Compassion is valuable currency anywhere in the world, but especially so in a place like Iraq, where there's still so much poverty. Displaced people inhabited pastiches of tents and aluminum siding. At one point, we passed by a shepherd boy, who looked liked he was around eight years old, bundled up in so many wool sweaters that he was almost indistinguishable from the hundreds of sheep around him.

Sulaiman shepherded as a boy, too, growing up in a village where his parents ran an apiary and traded cows, sheep, and goats. His respect for animals wasn't personal, he insisted, but religious. He explained how the Quran advises over many aspects of the treatment of animals, before listing some of them: do not alter the shape of an animal, such as cutting its tails or branding it; do not overload mules with loads heavier than their weight; do not slaughter pregnant animals, nor show the animals the knife you intend to slaughter it with, and you should slaughter it as quickly and painlessly as possible; do not destroy bird nests.

"So how come in the Muslim countries I've been to there are so many strays and starving animals?" I asked as inoffensively as I could. "Especially dogs."

"Animal rights in Quran are clear but now we are not following them," he said. "People say dogs are dirty animals, but the Quran never mentioned the dog is dirty. Maybe—I tell you this—maybe because, according to the messenger Prophet Muhammad, *alayhi s-salaam*, the angels cannot enter a home that has a dog."

I sat back to reflect on what Sulaiman said. The views he described were so different from my own, but I tried to put myself in the other person's shoes to see how someone could come to that conclusion.

My mind wandered back to a memory from a decade earlier. It was October 2000, and I'd driven home six hours from Edmonton for Thanksgiving. We were a family that loved camping outdoors, and growing up, I ate as much wild meat as I did store-bought. We would venture out into the wilderness's beauty for hours, and every time we did, my dad would impress upon me the importance of taking care of Mother Nature.

In my family's eyes, hunting was a way to eat meat while also getting out in nature. For my dad, like many other hunters, there was a way to be a good hunter and a bad one. To them, hunting had a strict ethical code. You had to show tremendous respect for the dignity of the animals and their environment, because you couldn't separate the meat you ate from the animal.

That day, we found a buck that we followed into a small clearing. My dad led the way, walking carefully so as not to crack the twigs or jostle branches, delicately trying to stalk the deer in the aspen forest. I mounted the rifle on my right shoulder, pushed the cold steel of the barrel against my cheek, shut my left eye, and aimed the barrel at the kill zone. The vital organs. The best chance at killing the deer in a clean shot.

My dad silently pushed my elbow up, straightening the scope with my eye line, metal pressed firmly around my eye socket, then slid my

baseball hat backward on my head. "Easy, Spencer, just squeeze the trigger," whispered my dad as he watched over my shoulder.

I exhaled as the muzzle exploded with a deafening crack and simultaneous kick from the gun that pushed my shoulder backward. The 150-pound, white-tail buck immediately jolted from the impact and sprinted off into the brush where it dropped into a tall bed of grass. The only visible part was its expansive antlers standing three feet above its head.

"Yes!" I exclaimed.

"Good shot!" said my dad, clapping me on the shoulder. He hurried off in the animal's direction.

I gave him my camera and posed with the antlers in my hands like I was steering a ship. Then, we lifted the deer by its legs onto the back of the pickup to drive back to the butcher.

At that point in my life, I'd killed far more creatures than I'd ever thought to adopt as a pet, and, although I was gradually developing different views from my family on some things, one thing we still agreed on was that domestic animals belonged outside. It wasn't an unusual outlook for families like mine. We'd never had pets, so I had no frame of reference—animals were animals, not companions.

I'd come a long way from those early hunting days to where I was now, sitting in the passenger seat beside Kurdistan's premier animal advocate. As the highway began to widen again, the sun dropped behind the mountains' frosted summits, casting a purple haze over the desert valley, where the Tigris River reflected the dusk's tangerine sun. Along the way, Sulaiman pointed his glowing cigarette out the window at Saddam Hussein's old palaces and landmarks of heinous acts ordered by the dictator, one after another, recalling the years when Hussein used Kurdistan as his personal playground. Near sundown, we pulled over for Sulaiman to pray at a mosque. The iridescent light of its minaret against the sunset filled me with a feeling of complete peace.

We stopped again to deliver my duffel bag to a refugee camp. It took all of a minute—I simply passed the bag to Kurdish soldiers at

the checkpoint two hundred meters from the tents and porta-potties so that they could disseminate the clothes peacefully. Give and release.

We finally arrived in Duhok around seven at night, by which point we were famished. Sulaiman took me to a humble restaurant. In the kitchen at the front of the restaurant, there were tubs of minced meat and a flaming grill covered in kebabs. It'd been a few years since I ate meat, and my taste for it had almost been fully extinguished since I'd made a vow of pescetarianism in 2009—a decision based primarily on ethics, not tastes. I could hear my lizard brain yelping with excitement at the sight of the kebabs. *Just to be polite*, I told my internal voice.

The plastic-wrapped tabletop quickly filled with spiced beef and chicken, bowls of soup and beans, plates of grilled tomatoes, fresh onions and hot peppers, and my Achilles' heel: warm bread. Though my athletic aspirations were long gone, I'd remained committed to trying to maintain a healthy body, so I tried to minimize complex carbohydrates and sugars. But I also knew that gluten-free wasn't much of an excuse in this part of the world.

Several rounds of food later, I put what I assumed was my last forkful of meat in my mouth, but before I could swallow, Sulaiman dropped another kebab on my plate. I tried to fend it off with my fork, but it was futile. I was adamant about not wasting food, a product of my upbringing. I routinely stopped students from throwing away a perfectly good sandwich and created a food basket in my classroom so that we could donate any food they didn't want to eat.

So I broke off another morsel of meat, reminding myself that I was a guest.

"How come you have no children?" Sulaiman asked. "Wife, but no kids. Why?"

"Our life is pretty amazing right now."

"But children are the vegetables of the home."

"I'm pretty sure vegetables are the vegetables of the home." I laughed through a full mouth. "How many kids do you have?"

He wiped his chin with a napkin nonchalantly. "Five." My eyes bulged and I lifted my fist to my mouth to help me swallow. "Next year, six."

Before the table was cleared, the server in a paper diner hat brought a tray of Turkish delights, halva, and baklava. Sulaiman pushed it toward me insistently—"eat, eat"—and I pushed it back with the balls of my palm.

"I don't want it."

"You don't know what you're missing," he said, popping a sweet in his mouth and reaching for a cigarette in one motion. Before I could protest, he picked up the tab, which somehow amounted to about ten dollars each, and then drove me to my hotel. I thanked him and arranged a time for us to meet the next morning so we could begin working before waving good night.

I wasn't expecting the Ritz, and I've certainly done my share of roughing it, but as I entered the hotel that Sulaiman had arranged for me, alarm bells started ringing. The lights were off on one side of the lobby and my room reeked. There were yellow streaks of nicotine on the wallpaper. But the final straw was when I opened my laptop to send an email home and discovered there was no Wi-Fi. I packed my computer bag and hauled my carry-on back downstairs, around the broken elevator, and asked for a room with internet. "There's Wi-Fi over there," said the man at the front desk, pointing to a corner of the dark lobby. I thanked him and walked right past the corner to the street outside, where I hailed a cab.

After a brief game of charades with a taxi driver, summoning my best pantomimes to represent "nice hotel," I was dropped off at the Dilshad Palace in the heart of the city. I pulled out a wad of Iraqi cash that made me feel like a millionaire, and peeled off five thousand dinars—about five bucks.

"No, no, no," said the cab driver, pressing his hand against his heart. "I cannot, I cannot."

"Thanks, buddy," I said, slapping him on the shoulder. I headed

inside with my bag, shaking my head in amazement at the driver's gesture of hospitality and generosity, one I experienced wherever I traveled in the Middle East. People's adamant refusal to charge money if they were helping someone in need—I'd once complimented someone's shirt and watched him offer to give it to me, right there, off his bare back—was something to behold.

Years later, another Middle Eastern friend of mine told me that I misunderstood the situation. The driver was practicing a custom of fake generosity called *taarof*. He was supposed to pretend he didn't want money, and I was supposed to insist he take it, and we were supposed to do this for upward of a minute before he finally accepted my money. Another lesson for another time, I suppose. If I ever meet that taxi driver again, though, I'll repay him with ten times the fare, because that split-second decision I made to get in his car, and his suggestion of that particular hotel, would alter the course of my life.

Chapter three

"Until one has loved an animal, a part of one's soul remains unawakened."

—ANATOLE FRANCE

The next day, Sulaiman brought me to his home. When we arrived, he unlocked a red gate and opened a garage door at the bottom of a tile staircase. "Hello," he greeted a black-and-white kitten crying with a crackly mew. He clicked his tongue at her and wiggled his foot to keep her from making a break for it between our legs. I shut the door behind me and looked around. The garage was big and sparse. The basics of pet care—leashes, flea collars, and toys—hung on a white wall.

"What's upstairs?" I asked.

"My family," said Sulaiman, pouring a cup of kibbles in a bowl by the kitten's litter box.

"Where's the clinic?"

Sulaiman gestured at the walls. Dr. Sulaiman Tameer didn't just create KOARP, he *was* KOARP. Sulaiman explained that he had a salary job doing policy consulting for Kurdish Environmental Affairs, but the work was tenuous and there was no money to implement his ideas. The financial resources to treat the volume of strays just didn't exist, so Sulaiman was working alone to implement a spay/neuter and vaccination program he'd learned about in Istanbul, Turkey. If there was a singular voice for animals in Kurdistan, this was it: a

forty-seven-year-old frenetic veterinarian treating homeless kittens in his garage.

I plopped my canvas bag onto the table and unloaded some supplies donated to me by a Canadian veterinarian before leaving. I stacked boxes of antibiotics, syringes, bandages, and medicine, but as Sulaiman added them to his cabinet stock it became obvious he was already well supplied. His bigger challenge was simply getting people to recognize the value of his work. In Iraq and other unstable regions, he explained, pet health was understandably fickle and those who did care about their animals' well-being would rather they reproduce than not. That was especially true of dogs, which were more likely to be a macho status symbol than a family member.

"My organization has no funding," Sulaiman said, leading me into the office with the kitten under his armpit like a football. "No—no—nobody give me anything. No government. So, say you come to me, say you have this cat. And you bring it, you say, 'I need a vaccine.' I give you it for $10. From that $10, maybe I make $2. But it isn't for me. That $2 is for the strays." He grabbed a vial off his cluttered desk and the kitten stopped crying seconds after he dropped antibiotics into her green eyes. She jumped off the desk onto a Persian rug, scratched the brown couch I was sitting on, and then hopped up. I saw one of her eyes was half-closed and infected. As she climbed into my lap, I instinctively recoiled, and then relaxed. I scratched under her chin, careful not to touch my eyes afterward lest I end up looking like her. I am incredibly allergic to cats and you would think I'd have learned long ago, but I still succumb to the great joy of hearing the rumble of their purr.

My bigger concern was the breakfast Sulaiman returned with: a massive platter of glistening chopped fruit and vegetables. My stomach was already miffed about the starches and meats from the night before, and I doubted it would forgive me for eating food washed in local water.

But Sulaiman wouldn't take no for an answer. "Eat, eat, please,

you must." He thrust an individual plate piled with peach slices, figs, and grapes toward me, the droplets splashing me. I said no, and he said no back.

"It's okay, one hundred percent good," he said.

Like I haven't heard that everywhere I've gotten sick before, I thought.

Sulaiman's insistence wore on me and sounded half-threatening, so I bit into a fig to appease him. I'd never tasted a fresh one before— it was a strange and seedy delight that seemed to muzzle my protesting stomach. I chewed it slowly while Sulaiman give me a tour of the literature he'd written, a mix of government strategies, children's books about animals, and even a history of the Kurdish people.

"I didn't realize you were a historian," I said, leafing the book with pages of Arabic script backward, from left to right, by habit of only ever reading the English language.

"It's been a very, very, very long time that we are suffering horrible conditions, Spencer," he said. "Not just treatment from the Iraqi people. Iran, Turkey, Syria. Each one was finding us and they kill us. But our culture is very, very strong. You need time to understand it." He put the history book at the top of a pile and placed the whole set in my bag. "For you," he said. I thanked him, wondering what I was going to do with five Kurdish-language books.

"Were you ever arrested?"

"Arrested?" His throat choked up and grumbled with mucus. He snorted it back up. "They shot me!"

Sulaiman's family had been effectively exiled from their home to Duhok in 1975, just after the Second Iraqi–Kurdish War. The conflict never really ended, so most of his male relatives joined the Kurdish defense army, the Peshmerga, who were training in Iran. But Sulaiman was intent on helping animals, even if studying veterinary medicine was a twelve-year process in Iraq. Still, as it is for virtually all Kurds, politics is personal. In 1991, when the Peshmerga returned from Iran to lead another uprising against Saddam Hussein's Ba'athists,

Sulaiman was amongst the first to march in Duhok's market square with other unarmed protesters to demand independence. Sulaiman was also amongst the first to experience the government's retaliation that early Wednesday morning when the Iraqi military met the protesters with live ammunition.

Sulaiman unbuttoned his checkered shirt and pulled up his undershirt to reveal a vertical scar above his pelvis. "After ten day in hospital, we went to the border of Turkey."

"Who?"

"Everyone—my family, all my neighbors. Duhok became empty. Just military, and they destroyed *allllll* the area. They found a district, or quarter, and bombed it. One is mine. One is my sister's. One is my cousin's."

I asked him how he got to Turkey. He said his father drove the family to the edge of the snow-draped mountains and got a donkey for Sulaiman's fevered body. His mom didn't even have shoes for the two-week journey to Turkey's Hakkâri Province.

"In Turkey, I had three operations because my body was like . . ." He trailed off, thinking of the right word. "Pus? You call it pus? Like cheese. All my body was like cheese!"

My jaw clenched, crunching a juicy grape that splashed in my mouth. Up until Sulaiman described his body so repulsively, I was rapt by his story. So rapt, I'd forgotten about my aversion to washed fruit and snacked on it like movie theater popcorn. I pushed my belly, feeling for any discomfort. So far, so good.

Finally, we headed out in his truck to Sulaiman's first case of the day. Because so few people knew about Sulaiman, or if they did, even thought to bring him in if they found an injured stray, he was constantly improvising. We drove along the brown countryside, stopping to inquire with shepherd boys about the possibility of stray dogs in the area. Two brothers in layers of sweaters took us to a makeshift cave in the side of a sandy bluff that a mama dog must have dug herself. The ground crumbled under our feet as we climbed the hill with

water jugs and an extra large kibble bag. The whole way up, Sulaiman made a curious puppy call: "*Yip, yip, yip, yip, yip.*"

The little mutts were asleep, folded into themselves and bundled together like a brown-and-white laundry load. Their mother was likely out hunting, but from the looks of their fine physical health and the nearby bones with meat on them, she was still in the picture. Sulaiman littered the area with a quarter of the kibble he had, and I filled a nearby plastic bin with water. Unlike the urban areas of Kurdistan, the countryside was strewn with trash that made it easy for stray dogs to become scavengers and a nuisance to people. "All the time, I tell the municipality, 'Please control the garbage.' But no one listens to me," Sulaiman complained to me on the way down the hill.

The shepherds took us to a second litter born under a metal cargo container raised on blocks in the desert. I tried my best to step around the prickly plants, but my shins were adorned with sharp burrs by the time we got to the mass of puppies. They were a mix of colors—tan, black-and-white, or tinged dark brown—and they wriggled in the sand with barely open eyes, emitting the sweetest puppy moans. I couldn't help myself from trying to hold one.

"Wait," said Sulaiman, blocking my reach with his smoking hand. He put the cigarette between his lips and pulled latex gloves from his kit. I wore them to appease the doctor, but ended up smooching the puppy anyway. A white blaze ran down its forehead to the tip of its nose and formed a white bib in the shape of a cross on its neck. I picked up another, a chocolate mutt with white boots. I pressed my lips and nose into its soft fur and whiffed the puppy with enjoyment. Despite a few burrs in their coats, the dogs were in no immediate peril and appeared well fed.

Suddenly, we were alerted by aggressive barking to our right. It was Mom, looking none too happy with us near her brood. I placed the puppy gently with its siblings and held them in place while Sulaiman gave them each a booster shot. We peeled off our gloves, shook the young shepherds' hands, and started back to the truck.

As I sank into the seat, I felt my belly grumble. It was clearly angry about my last two days of dietary decisions, especially that morning's, but I forgot about it as soon as we pulled into a kerosene station that had requested Sulaiman's services. The shop's guard dog needed flea control, multivitamins, seven vaccines, and a legal certificate clearing it of rabies suspicions. All for 70,000 dinars—or $60.

Standing in the shade of a cement building, four Kurdish guys drank tea, smoked shisha, and thumbed their phones. There was a scattering of oil drums, tools, and pipes, and a skinny white dog chained to a doghouse by a tight leash. While Sulaiman went to the men, I immediately took to the dog, and her to me. The men gawked at me while she licked my face and I laughed. They were somewhat mesmerized, somewhat repulsed. Some Muslims believe dog saliva is so filthy that anywhere on your skin that it licks needs to be sanitized with dirt.

"Spencer," Sulaiman called back, "be careful, because yesterday it bite him." I looked at the man in question—he was young, healthy, standing straight, breathing, and doing fine, so I ignored the warning and continued nuzzling the dog.

"You're a sweetheart, aren't you?" I said before turning to one of the guys sitting around.

"What's her name?"

"Lucy." She was not much more than a puppy, a husky mix with white, clean, and healthy looking teeth, but she was made for colder climates, and I pitied her for the ramshackle version of a doghouse they kept her in. There was a larger fenced-off area with good shade by the cement building. I asked Sulaiman to tell them in Kurdish that it would be a healthier environment for Lucy. She could roam around in the shaded, fenced area.

Sulaiman spoke with the men, but I don't think my message got through. I stepped aside to let Sulaiman do his work, thinking to myself that, in many ways, the feral dogs had it better than their domesticated counterparts. But I had to remind myself that as much as I

wanted to help Lucy, I was coming into someone else's country. It was not my place to convince them to treat animals according to my Western standards unfamiliar to them. I believed these animals were meant to roam and run, not to spend life on the end of a chain, and they believed otherwise.

As I got back into Sulaiman's truck, my chest felt hollow. I knew I'd never see Lucy again. I'd only just met her, but I couldn't help but feel that I was abandoning her. I was here to help these animals, but I felt as though my hands were tied. I was an outsider looking in—how was I going to make a difference?

Other than a stray cat that showed up at our house for a short period when I was a boy, I'd never had a pet as a kid. So in 2000, when my girlfriend at the time suggested we get a dog, I was hesitant. I knew that getting a pet together was a symbolic statement of commitment, one I wasn't prepared to make, even though I was in my midthirties. I tried to mitigate the burden by suggesting we adopt a smaller breed or one prone to lethargy like, say, a mastiff or a Great Dane. But it was hopeless. We adopted Chloe, an Alaskan malamute, a dog bred to mush through snowy northern tundra and the furthest thing from low-maintenance.

Chloe would grow into a hulking creature capable of pulling even me through the snow, but she arrived a delicate, ten-week-old snuggle-monger, and my resentment quickly gave way to affection beyond my control. That I came home stressed out from the changes in my teaching job didn't matter to her. Regardless of how good or bad my day may have been, the moment I walked in the door, she would erupt in a full-body wag, ears pinned down with happiness, as though every afternoon was the best one of her life. She asked for so little—a daily run, a steady walk, food, and a home—and in return, she showed me love and loyalty like I'd never felt before.

Indeed, Chloe changed every texture of my life, and before long, I evolved into the guy who unconsciously spewed a stream of baby talk

to random dogs on sidewalks. A lump would rise in my throat upon hearing stories of animal rescues or abuse, and I started volunteering at my local humane society.

The relationship with my girlfriend ended before Chloe's second birthday. We argued over who had rights over which DVDs, appliances, and furniture, but there was no question as to who would get full custody of Chloe. I was thankful that I still had Chloe in my life, but taking care of her by myself was harder than I'd thought. I was still working two jobs to make ends meet, so after coming home, there was hardly enough time to feed her and go for a run before leaving again. Even though Chloe had a dog door to the yard, her sad eyes beckoned to me through a fence hole as I walked to my truck every morning for work. Here I was, entrusted with the life of this animal who showed me nothing but devotion. I wanted to show her at least the same level of consideration. So I did something I'd never have imagined I would do: I got another dog.

I named my second malamute Mac, after the tallest mountain in North America, Mount McKinley in the Alaska Range. Though he quickly grew into the name, Mac remained sweet and docile, rolling onto his back submissively to Chloe, who evolved into a schoolyard bully. She never hesitated to take the food right out his bowl or, without seemingly any notice or provocation, ignite some terrible-sounding fight with him. Yet she remained terrified of hot-air balloons—despite her strength and fearlessness, when she saw one in the sky, she would go absolutely insane and begin to wail and try to hide, tail stuck deep between her legs.

As anyone living in a multipet household will tell you, adding more than one animal in the mix amplifies the personality of each. But Chloe, Mac, and I thrived together. I'd never before thought it possible to form intense bonds with another species, but Chloe and Mac slipped themselves into every part of my life with those beautiful golden eyes. At times, I even wondered if it was possible to share this honesty and vulnerability I felt with other humans.

One spring day in 2003, I took the pack to an off-leash dog park by the North Saskatchewan River, where I met a woman walking a rescue dog named Keena. The dog, a "Heinz 57," had golden-colored fur and a round body that resembled a sausage more than a canine. The dog's eyes would have been hard to look away from were it not for those of the gorgeous, tall, brown-haired woman with a big, warm smile beside her. I came to the same park every day, but I hadn't seen her before. We chatted for a while about our dogs, like two parents with strollers in the park, desperate for an engaged listener to hear all about our fur kids' shenanigans. And then we said goodbye.

A few days later, I ran into Keena's "mom," whose name I'd forgotten, again. *Karen, was it?* I thought when I saw her across the park. We continued talking about each other's dog and not much else. "I grew up with a malamute," she said, her hands scratching under the chins of both of my dogs, "so I'm extra drawn to these guys." Chloe, as she was prone to do, towered over Keena, pushing her protruded chest into Keena's personal space, raising her tail, and tensing her body to intimidate the poor rotund dog. As my furry beast walked away, the woman noticed, "She's limping."

"Yeah, she does that sometimes," I said. "Don't know what it is, but it just goes and comes back, goes and comes back. The anti-inflammatory medicine upsets her stomach and only works for a little while."

"Maybe I can help. I'm a chiropractor—I can make an adjustment." I knew embarrassingly little of chiropractic, and Keena's mom could read that ignorance on my face. "All it means is putting small force to a specific spot to move her joint into a normal position."

I had tried everything else and had nothing to lose so I shrugged my shoulders and said, "Go ahead."

I sat in the grass and hugged Chloe's head from the front while the woman bent over her back and held her right foreleg with both hands. "Will this hurt?" I asked. She shook her head no and told me to hold tight. She thrust upward toward herself and Chloe let out

a quick, almost indistinguishable yelp and wiggled free. As she ran toward Mac, the limp was gone. I never saw it again.

Somehow, I never thought to re-ask this savior for her name.

"I just want to say thank you for helping Chloe," I said. "I really appreciate the help, Karen."

"Don't mention it," she said. "Although, just so you know—my name's Christie."

I immediately flushed red. Luckily, I had plenty of chances to make up for it, as I ran into Christie almost every day after that. Little did I know, Christie had adjusted something else—Keena's walking schedules—to the same time as mine every day, hoping to run into me at the park. We exchanged numbers and became fast friends.

Christie, like me, grew up in a small town before moving to Edmonton. By twenty-six, she had her own successful clinic, but she was so busy building a practice that she'd put little effort into building romantic relationships. Only now, with her clinic on the verge of really thriving, did she have time to adopt a dog and, maybe, a boyfriend? But I couldn't. I wouldn't. Our friendship was too solid, unlike any I'd had before, and I was warned by many of my friends that "the perfect couple" is very rare.

"We get along really well," I told Christie one night at my house, where she'd brought two candles to light while we watched the hockey game on TV. "Why ruin it?"

I was back to being a consummate bachelor and didn't feel in a rush to bring an end to that lifestyle. In hindsight, I was reaching the point where, if I'd been single much longer, I might have become weirdly self-centered and frivolous. I am grateful to this day that Christie pulled me back from that.

A few months later, Christie went on a weekend trip with her girlfriends. We were only apart for a few days, but the short time away made me realize that she was everything I had ever wanted in a life partner. I decided right then I would try to be the man of her dreams when she got back.

Despite my fear of losing someone who'd become an amazing friend, I took the plunge and initiated "the talk" that turned our friendship into a romantic relationship. I'd waited for someone like Christie my whole life and felt like I had to make up for lost time.

For Christie's thirtieth birthday, I got her thirty cards, one for every birthday I'd missed and inscribed each one with something special about her:

> *You've brought so much happiness and joy into my life, more than you'll ever know or I can ever say.*

> *You don't argue when I tell you you're beautiful.*

> *I love everything about you, Christie. Your funniness, silliness, your loyalty, your trust, your values, your honesty, your goals.*

Most of all, though, I loved Christie's patience. For better or worse, I could be a reactive force that needed someone to talk through my problems with me or talk me down from my own volatility. Often those moments started with a frantic phone call.

"Christie! I lost your dog," went one of those calls.

"What do you mean?" Christie asked. She was between patients without much time to talk, let alone problem-solve a lost dog, but she remained cool-headed for the both of us.

"I don't know. I put her in the truck and drove away, and she's not in here anymore."

"What was the last thing you did before you drove off?"

"Nothing, I packed the dogs in the backseat, then I saw this other dog and—" I replayed the scene in my head. The puppy in the park was so cute that I lost time petting it and talking with the owner. I'd been so caught up in this random dog that I must have missed Keena leaping out of the window. Where that plump animal found the athleticism to pull that feat off still baffles me to this day. Luckily, she

didn't get far, and I tracked her down wandering amiably around the park.

Another time I was out for a bike ride with Mac and Chloe when I saw something crash through the brush nearby. I turned around and immediately pulled out my phone.

"Christie! There's a moose after me!"

"Don't call me, call the moose police," she said. "I'll get you the number."

The fact that Christie didn't block my number after each call was a solid indication that I'd struck the jackpot.

Things tend to move fast in my world. And when you know, you know. On our first Valentine's Day as a couple, we followed a romantic dinner with our evening winter routine of dog sledding. Little did Christie know that Mac and Chloe were my coconspirators in an elaborate proposal, along with a lifelong friend who had lit up dozens of tea lights in paper bags in the shape of a heart and spray-painted "Christie, will you marry me?" in the snow.

We joined our packs and transformed our three dogs into ring-bearers that summer, in 2004. It still seems incredible to me that animals could so dramatically steer my life in a once inconceivable direction. Once again, my world was expanding in the most remarkable ways, and my new pack would continue to be my compass for years to come.

"Christie . . ."

"Did you drink the water again?"

I lay naked in a fetal position on my hotel bed in Duhok in a cold sweat. Earlier that afternoon, death had started hovering over me and Sulaiman had rushed me back to my room, fearing the bacteria I'd ingested would evacuate from both ends soon. Of course, he insisted that we stop at the nearby zoo along the way to discuss some business with the zoo owner, Ramadan Hassan Salim. He tried to introduce

me to Ramadan, but I was in no condition for a long chat. I gave Ramadan a quick handshake by the front gate and then retreated to the truck.

"You have to let your stomach rest," Christie reminded me. "Don't eat again until you're rehydrated and feel better."

"I'll never trust another drop of water."

"You might have to," she said with her big smile. "Just make sure it's from a bottle this time."

I could feel another evacuation on its way and I didn't want to bring her with me, but I couldn't let go of Christie's image. Looking at my pale, perspiring face, Christie frowned. "Here," she said, turning the selfie feature on her camera off and showing me our malamutes sleeping on the couch.

Sadly, Keena had died two years before, but Mac ran toward my face with his thick legs flailing wildly and whole body vibrating. I was instantly energized. "Hello, little buddy," I said giddily, momentarily forgetting that my intestines were at war.

I followed Christie's advice and let my stomach rest and slowly rehydrated myself with bottled water and salt crackers from the minibar in between naps. I then called room service to request the most expensive bananas I'd ever ordered. Slowly, my body warmed up and my skin stopped perspiring. By six o'clock that evening, I wasn't feeling 100 percent, but I was well enough to leave the hotel for a walk and make the best of my short time in the city.

Duhok is a spread-out city, taupe and arid. Many of the half-finished buildings in every direction looked abandoned. The only trees I could see were landscaped palms running down the center of a thoroughfare. The traffic was heavy, but the only other pedestrians were two young men, walking with their arms around each other's shoulders—not an unusual sight in the Middle East, where, despite their machismo, young men are unabashedly and platonically affectionate. I stopped at a grocery store for another banana and chewed it slowly as I strolled aimlessly.

I spotted a sign with lions, zebras, and giraffes and an arrow pointing toward the zoo where Sulaiman and I had stopped earlier. While the rest of the city felt like it was created with a limited paint swatch ranging from cream to beige, the Duhok Zoo entrance was an explosion of colors and energy, complete with its own waterfall. The teenager working the ticket booth recognized me as Dr. Tameer's assistant and waved me in. I walked along a shaded path beneath speakers emitting Middle Eastern children's music. It was eerily quiet except for the looping tune and roosters calling from the grassy quad, roaming around an inflatable jumpy castle.

The first enclosure I came across was a parrots' cage. The ground inside it was littered with juice boxes and pistachio shells. I picked an unshelled nut off the ground and held it in place for one of the birds. It slowly stretched its cracked tongue through the bars and took the nut, but it wouldn't stick and the nut dropped to the ground.

They must be thirsty. Sure enough, their water feeders were dry, so I went to the canteen for a bottle of water. As I entered, a kid, no older than ten, was running away from his register to the back of the shop, saying, "*Na, na, na.*" I followed him to the fracas: a baby chimpanzee in a striped red sweater and blue shorts was raiding all the goodies from the bottom two shelves. The boy tore a couple of taffy bars from the chimp's wrinkly hands, so the chimp gnawed a package of savory pumpkin seeds instead, spilling them onto the floor and shoveling them into its mouth.

The zoo owner, Ramadan, came running in. "Manno, no," he cried. He managed to grab the chimp's two hands, holding them in the air to restrain the rambunctious animal. The chimp curled his legs up and joyously swung like an acrobat.

Then Ramadan, a tall man with a shaved head wearing a black mock turtleneck and faded jeans, placed Manno in my arms.

I looked around. *Did he mean to give me the chimp?* Sure enough, Ramadan was offering me the chimpanzee. I crouched and the little guy wrapped his hairy arms around my neck and his legs around my

waist. He looked into my eyes, breathing softly through his big, wing-shaped nostrils, and then nuzzled my neck.

"What's his name?" I asked the kid. He didn't answer because he'd already gone to get a broom. I stood alone in the mess, combing the back of the chimp's head gently with my fingers. "What's your name, little man?"

Chapter four

"It is never too late to be what you might have been."

—GEORGE ELIOT

When Manno looked at me with those soulful golden-brown eyes, his ears pressed against my chest, there was no place I would rather be. I spent the rest of that evening carting him around the zoo, cuddling him under my coat as he slept. I tried to think about how I'd describe the experience to Christie. Manno couldn't have weighed more than ten or fifteen pounds, as much as a small dog. Once Manno latched on to me, Ramadan and the other attendants became invisible to him, which the staff didn't seem to mind. They loved Manno deeply, but it was also apparent that they were relieved to have a break from chasing the bundle of mischief around the grounds.

Despite the peace that evening, something didn't sit well with me. After the last family left the zoo and it was time for staff to lock up, the overnight attendant called me over. I reluctantly gave up Manno to the attendant, who coaxed Manno into a rectangular, black-wire cage. Suddenly, Manno turned feral, screaming and flailing like the wild animal he was, not the baby like which he was treated. He tried to bite the attendant as he clamped the latch. I couldn't explain the change in behavior, but then I saw that Manno's cage was propped on top of a wooden box that housed snakes overnight, triggering biological terror.

Before moving Manno's cage from there to a wood hut—the same

one where the attendant slept on a cot—the man shook my hand and thanked me. It was then that I realized that I'd benefited from a bit of mistaken identity. The zoo staff seemed to have assumed I was a veterinarian or zoologist because I'd first visited with Sulaiman. Judging by the foreigners I'd met in the hotel elevator, Kurdistan seemed full of European and American professionals working for charitable groups. It wouldn't have occurred to the zoo staff, then, that I was a social studies teacher who was there as a volunteer. I wasn't about to break up the charade and, in the process, lose the experience of a lifetime that afforded me full access to caring for this baby chimpanzee. I was completely entranced by this small, humanlike creature. To say that I fell in love with Manno is the truth. Even in those very first moments, I never saw him as just an animal. I saw a sentient being; I saw a little soul. I saw a friend.

I quickly became a fixture at the zoo. Sulaiman's government contract required him to do a slew of facility inspections at slaughterhouses and ranches. We fell into a daily routine—while Sulaiman worked at his government job each morning, I went to visit Manno at the zoo. After my morning workout and breakfast, I walked to the zoo and entered under the faux-stone arch. I passed the ticket booth and listened for Manno. I learned to anticipate what his mood would be based on the calls he was making. Distinct squeals and panting hoots—something like hyperventilating laughter—meant he was in a good mood; crashing, banging, and the sound of admonishment showed he was feeling the opposite. Either way, though, the moment Manno saw me, he barreled toward me and leapt off his knuckles into my arms.

Manno was hyperaware of humans and yet seemed oblivious to the other caged animals, even the peacocks and roosters roaming freely. It was the same in reverse. Perhaps it was the roughly 98 percent DNA we shared, but I hardly noticed the other animals when he was around. Other visitors felt the same—the moment they spotted the diapered primate, they made a beeline to pet him and coo, often getting lost in his gaze. Manno, however, didn't love the attention, and he was prone to scratching and biting the guests.

Whenever I handed Manno over to an attendant or to Ramadan, he would throw a tantrum, refusing to let go of me and squealing with outstretched, lanky arms until I took him back. When he wasn't snuggled over my shoulders, he was sprinting around the grounds, chomping into books and plastic water bottles, leaping across sofas and tables in the offices, or charging into the zoo canteen and turning it upside down. A spoiled toddler incapable of following a single command, Manno, given any opportunity, was determined to get into *something*.

Manno wasn't the only zoo resident who could be difficult. One morning, one of the smaller monkeys—all of whom were kept in wicker baskets overnight—had escaped and was creating mayhem. The thin, black macaque swung over to me, and I gazed up at the tiny creature as it inched closer.

"How are you, little fella?" I asked in baby talk. He immediately swung down from the rafters of the roof and sat at my feet. I squatted in front of him, and his tiny, leathery hands explored and caressed my face. I laughed as he playfully tugged at my lips with his hands, but then he surprised me by sticking his hands in my mouth, pulling at my tongue, and quizzically exploring my oral cavity. I giggled a little. *He really likes me*, I thought.

Then, just as quickly as he descended, the monkey scampered back up to a ledge above my head. I stood up, smiling at the playful, interspecies interaction. *Looks like I've got another friend.* But then I noticed a dark mass protruding from the macaque's backside. Using the same hand that had just been tugging at my lips and tongue, the monkey reached around, grabbed the feces from his bum, and casually flung it onto the ground in front of me.

I grunted in disgust and instinctively began spitting and coughing to try and remove the foulness that I realized had just entered my mouth. How could I be so stupid?

Ramadan trained me on how to change Manno's diapers. It was about the only time Manno treated me as an adversary, folding forward and biting my fingers as I tried to clean him. Manno was

probably only ten months old, so it was cute and harmless at the time, but it broke my heart to think about what might happen when he was older and too aggressive to coddle.

Every day with Manno in that zoo was a learning experience. Each night, I would pick Sulaiman's brain with questions about caring for primates, zoo regulations, and anything else that came to mind. I wasn't there to be a vet, though—I didn't have the training to do that. I knew where my limits lay. My last experience with caring for primates had taught me plenty on that front.

In 2011, I had spent some time at a sanctuary for bonobos, or pygmy chimps, in the Democratic Republic of the Congo. The sanctuary, Lola ya Bonobo, was founded by a Belgian woman, Claudine Andre, who rescued bonobos from captivity in hopes of returning the animals to the wild. It was usually a happy, if not calming, place. But the day that I arrived, there was a tragedy. A troop of the apes attacked two workers as they were released from their enclosure. The men had been severely wounded and required facial reconstructive surgery. That remained on my mind the rest of my stay at the sanctuary.

When I arrived at the sanctuary, I had first noticed the beautiful stone buildings that were once the country home of the country's former dictator Mobutu Sese Seko. As I climbed up sandy steps held in place by planks of wood, I noticed black creatures frolicking in the distance. Lola ya Bonobo was like an etiquette school that taught the orphaned animals how to be apes again after years of being raised in captivity by humans, dressed up in diapers and toddler clothes. Many of the apes ended up in the sanctuary after they grew too old for their owners' liking and no longer resembled the sweet babies their owners thought they'd be forever. Mature bonobos can have the strength and aggression of four men, and the sanctuary offered them a place to rehabilitate and live out their lives in peace.

The human-ape relationship is a complex one. Well-adjusted

bonobos who were properly rehabilitated could show tenderness to nonthreatening people. But if rehabilitation didn't work, it usually meant the animal was spoiled, unable to learn social cues about hierarchy and dominance, and they were often savagely beaten by other bonobos until they learned to submit.

When I arrived at the sanctuary, I had little experience to draw from, and I found the bonobos unpredictable. On one hand, there were gentle apes like Kipolo and Lukuru. Kipolo was a blind orphan who would reach through the bars and sweetly explore and caress every crevice of my face with his leathery hands as if to memorize who I was, only to cower and ball up when other, more aggressive bonobos would rush over and abuse him. And Lukuru was delightfully charming. When she saw me approaching the enclosure, she'd immediately rush over and hop up on the bars at head height. She'd push her belly against the green metal, inviting me to tickle her, all the while periodically checking over her shoulder to ward off a potential onslaught from other jealous apes. I would shower her with a flurry of noises and scratches, and she would squeal with absolute glee when I playfully tickled her ribs with my fingers.

Some apes, though, were more predictably unpredictable. Shibo was perhaps the norm—a mischievous, for lack of a better term, bully I met almost as soon as I arrived. I found Shibo in one of the four large enclosures filled with hay.

"Hey little buddy," I said. I approached cautiously and kept the enclosure's bars between us, having been warned by a keeper who was missing some digits that Shibo could sometimes react violently. I thought I was a safe distance away, when suddenly, as quick as an Ali jab, Shibo's hand slipped between the bars and smacked my chin with a fierce uppercut, leaving my face raw and tingling from the impact. On another occasion, he stuck his belly out against the cage, acting like Lukuru miming for tickles. I thought it was an attempt to make friendly amends, so I cautiously reached out to tickle him. He seemed to be enjoying my attention, and for a moment, I thought

I had misjudged the little scamp. Then, I felt something warm and wet splashing on my feet. It took a moment for me to register what it was. As I looked down to witness the yellow stream splattering on my sandals and drenching my bare feet, Shibo reached through the bars, grabbed my shirt, and slammed me into the cage, the metal reverberating with the impact of my face against the cold steel bars.

The ape that Manno most reminded me of, though, was Kasai, a baby bonobo named after a tributary to the Congo River. Kasai was too weak to be with the other young bonobos at the sanctuary's "kindergarten" and was still so sweet. One time, while Christie and I were talking on Skype, I showed Christie's face to Kasai on my iPad, and Kasai covered the screen in kisses, smudging Christie's face.

Kasai was attached to a surrogate human who carried her around the jungle in a baby carrier. The surrogate was a motherly substitute who would be with Kasai literally every second of the day until she was strong enough to be introduced to the younger members of the troop through what they called "bonobo kindergarten." Over my week at the sanctuary, I spent hours with Kasai snuggling her in her diapers, letting her sleep in my lap, and feeding her. When I kissed her goodbye, I wondered whether she'd ever be able to adjust to the other rambunctious bonobos. She seemed so small and fragile. Sadly, she never got the chance, because five months later a flu swept through the sanctuary, killing her and a number of other orphans. My heart immediately sank when I heard the news at my home in Edmonton. I looked at the message over and over again in hopes that I had somehow read it incorrectly. I thought back on my time with Kasai, marveling at how fortunate I had been to share some time with that special little girl and yet despondent that an animal I had become so fond of had passed away as an infant.

My time in the Congo showed me just how necessary sanctuaries were in helping to protect apes. In the years since, I'd continued my

education and learned that bonobos were actually *less* aggressive than chimps, so even as I carried Manno around in my jacket or changed his diapers, I knew that his life in the Duhok Zoo wasn't sustainable.

There's no way anyone can truly tame apes. They are just too intelligent, strong, and unpredictable. Much as we giggle at entertainment chimps, the ones we see in videos riding tricycles or scooting around on skateboards—always in human clothes and grinning widely—that's a life chimps will only tolerate as juveniles. By the time they hit puberty, around seven or eight, they're impossible to handle. Deadly even.

I knew one thing for certain: if Manno wasn't taken to safety, his future was grim, and both he and his caregivers would be at risk. Eventually, his world would be reduced to a cement prison cell no bigger than a living room—a tragic place for an animal capable of empathy, altruism, communication, and other intellectual markers scientists are just beginning to understand. I'd only known Manno for a few days, but that wasn't a future I wanted for him.

On December 30, the day before my departure, I was awoken at *fajr*, the early morning prayer. The *adhan*, a slow, melodic call to worship, set off from one mosque, building with each minaret speaker for miles until I was immersed in a dreamlike song seemingly echoing from the black sky. I was eager to see Manno one last time before I left. I gulped down a drink with protein powder and snatched a banana from a bowl in the hotel lobby on my way out the door. Sunlight was just cracking the horizon when I arrived at the zoo gates. In my mind, I imagined attendants arriving hours before visitors to prepare buckets of feed, hose down the cages, and groom the ponies. But when I stuck my head through the bars, I saw nobody inside and heard nothing. I shook the gate. It was about eight feet high and flat across the top—no barbed wire to keep me from gripping the top bar and boosting myself up halfway. Looking around, I spotted two security officers parked outside with machine guns slung over their shoulders,

looking at me with familiarity. An old hockey mantra from Wayne Gretzky came to my mind—"You miss 100 percent of the shots you don't take"—and I locked my left leg against the fake stone arch and hoisted myself over the gate.

From their car, the security guards nodded their heads at me as if to say hello, not *Hey, you, get back over here!* You'd have thought a blond, fair-skinned man in the Muslim world would be a suspicious sight. But they'd seen me there almost every day and probably just assumed that I'd forgotten my keys to the zoo.

I squinted through a smudged window into the hut where Manno slept. He was rolled in a ball on a pile of cloth at the base of the cage. The attendant lay on a cot beside him. Not wanting to wake either one of them, I decided to give myself an intimate tour of the zoo. I stepped behind the protective fence that surrounded the various exhibits and made my way, reminding myself to stay alert. I'd seen enough YouTube videos of what could go wrong when a zoo visitor got too close to the bars.

I walked the perimeter of the 20,000-square-meter zoo, a spacious luxury compared to most zoos I'd seen in the developing world. The size didn't necessarily amount to tons more space for the animals, though. It just meant more animals, some of which puzzled me in their mundanity. A scruffy Persian cat with matted, dirty white fur mewed at me from the caged window of a shed, close to a row of domestic purebred dogs lapping water from a bowl. There was no doubt in my mind anymore that, in Kurdistan, it was better to be a stray roaming the countryside with your buddies and scavenging for food than to be "owned."

A little ways away, a baboon shredded toilet paper while another with a baby clinging to her belly chewed into a plastic bottle with her spike-like canines. There was little greenery, burrowing space, or even dirt on the floor to simulate the wild. A little farther along, lion cubs limped toward me across concrete, which is terrible for their joints. A leopard baby tried to paw me through the bars with no

claws out—just a kitten wanting to play—but I kept a close eye on the adult leopard striding from one wall to the other at the far end of the enclosure, who I sensed also wanted something to play with, albeit with sinister intentions.

In the adjacent cage, two wolves did the same thing, pacing back and forth over a pile of bones, as if trying to trick themselves into thinking they had more than fifteen feet of freedom. The bigger wolf noticed me and approached, pressing his wet nose through the bars and sniffing me. I crouched and slowly leaned toward him with my hands out.

"Easy, boy," I said. I was close enough to feel his cold nose on my cheek and sense his affection.

The animals didn't look starved. They didn't appear to be wounded. And truthfully, I'd seen smaller and dirtier enclosures in other countries. But it was the concrete floors and lack of objects or social stimulation for these animals that really gutted me. Manno, no doubt, had the richest social life and most freedom of all the animals there (until he was coaxed into his cage each night). But, again, what would happen when he was nearly four feet tall, pulsing with testosterone, and five times stronger than the people who might try to hug him? Imagine having to live out the rest of your life incarcerated in a small cell because you outgrew your cuteness?

Remembering I still had a banana in my bag, I returned to the baboons chewing on toilet paper and plastic. I held the fruit between the bars. The mother with her baby gently took the fruit, as if it were offered by an old friend. The big male didn't take to that kindly, though, and he lunged at her with a piercing scream that sent me back against the security barrier. He grabbed the other baboon by her gray mane and swung her to the wall, sending her baby flying and skidding across the floor. The mother scurried to her baby, screaming back at the male, and huddled with the infant while the assailant swallowed the banana in one bite. I immediately felt stupid. There was a reason why guests weren't supposed to feed the animals.

The overnight attendant, awoken by the chaos, stepped out of the hut in jeans and a sweater in the sunshine, stretching and yawning. He waved at me cordially, not at all suspicious or concerned that I was stalking the grounds alone before the gate was unlocked.

"*Salam 'alaykum*," I said, approaching him from across the quad.

"*Assalamu alaykum*."

"Manno?" I pointed inside the hut and then to myself. "Can I go see Manno?"

"*Temam*," he said with a head nod.

Manno was just waking up, his eyes rolling slowly in his head as he took in his surroundings, too tired to register me at first. I unlatched the door and scooped him up by the armpits while his arms reached for my protein shake. *Why not?* I thought. It had more nutritional value than the junk food he'd been eating from the canteen. He slurped the pink liquid and offered me a drink.

"Thanks," I said. "You're a good friend."

Shortly after nine, Ramadan arrived in a polo shirt and leather shoes. I'd interacted with him a few times by then, all of it limited to hand gestures and a handful of English words he understood. He was a gracious man, but a stoic one.

I had learned from Sulaiman that Ramadan had built, furnished, and inhabited the Duhok Zoo with his own funds. The only government assistance he'd received was the land. The municipality gave it to him in 2001 in hopes of creating a tourist attraction. The Iraq War made for some difficult years, but the subsequent economic boom for Kurdistan helped the zoo to grow, eventually becoming Iraq's second largest zoo after Baghdad.

I was sympathetic to Ramadan. When Ramadan was a child, his father, a schoolteacher, had always brought animals home—pigeons, rabbits, antelopes, peacocks, and an Indian monkey that lived with him like a house cat. They called the monkey Manno. That Ramadan would name a baby chimp after a cherished childhood pet suggested his affection was more than feigned. He was clearly a man who loved

animals, like me, even if we expressed it differently—him as a businessman, me as an activist.

I greeted Ramadan with Manno perched on my forearm, nestling against my chest. "I have a question for you," I said.

"Yes."

"Manno—where is he from?"

"I buy."

"I know, but where. Africa? Europe?"

"Ah," he said and gestured for me to follow him. His office was tidy and furnished with brown couches and marble tiles. There was a portrait of Prime Minister Nechirvan Barzani on one wall—paying respects to the Barzani clan was not unusual, whether in the airport, a supermarket, or a private home—and on the other, a photo of his father in military garb.

Ramadan turned on the air-conditioning and handed me a pen and a yellow Duhok Zoo receipt pad with translucent animals at the top of each page.

"Manno," he said, "fifteen thousand."

"American dollars?" I asked.

"Yes."

I wrote $15,000 in the price column. I had no frame of reference, but that didn't sound like much to me. "From where?" Beside Manno's name, I scribbled the route Ramadan said Manno took to get here: *Congo–Syria–Baghdad–Duhok.*

According to Ramadan, Syria had been only a stopover for Manno. He wasn't born there in captivity and, given his age when he arrived in Duhok two months ago, must have been moved through it rather quickly. *Was he smuggled?* Chimps are, after all, endangered—critically endangered if they're from the West African species. Then again, if Ramadan were part of a shady enterprise, surely he'd know better than to spell out the scheme for a strange, white "American." There must be another explanation.

"What about the other animals?" I asked. "Jaguar. Tiger. Elephant."

He nodded and dictated to me:

(2) $35,000 JAGUAR, Amazon–Italy–Istanbul–Duhok
(2) $25,000 TIGER, Istanbul–Duhok
(2) $100,000 LION, Congo–Syria–Duhok

I tore off the page and gave the stationery back to Ramadan. He started writing other animals—anacondas, baboons, zebras, even Rottweilers—the prices shrinking as he listed them. He stopped bothering with the routes, assuming maybe that I, like him, cared more about the costs. Ramadan flipped the sheet over and continued scribbling figures: 2 *elephant $6,000,000, 2 giraffe $4,000,000.* I hadn't seen an elephant or a giraffe anywhere, so I gathered he was pricing them out for me, showing me hypotheticals. The numbers were so astronomical that I had to assume he was accidentally adding extra zeros to them. Then again, what did I know about the exotic animal trade?

Soon enough, there was a four-page list of every animal a zoo-owner could want, itemized and priced like a quote, folded in my pocket. I looked it over while I lay on the attendant's cot in the hut and Manno climbed all over me, clambering onto the sink and atop the cage, then leaping back onto my chest. I grunted and Manno pant-laughed with a massive grin.

"So, you're from the Congo," I said. "How did they get you out?"

I imagine it began in the lush equatorial jungle: the Congo Basin. Five hundred million acres that cover half the country and span across five others. Tropical rainforest—umbrella-like crowns of moabi trees intertwined with the branches of mango, legume, and hundreds of other tree species—stretching up the mountainsides and down the Congo River valleys. Their leaves rustle with bonobos, five species of gorilla, and three subspecies of chimps as they leap and climb, forage and sleep, and hide from their predators. Big cats like leopards can

pounce and tear their necks open in a flash. Eagles might take a baby in their talons without a fight. But the greatest threat, of course, is a bipedal species bearing a striking resemblance to the chimps themselves.

If I was to believe Ramadan, and Ramadan was to believe his dealers, then Manno was probably from the eastern chimpanzee genus, *P. t. schweinfurthii*, in the north Democratic Republic of the Congo. He would have lived in a family of about ten. Because his family was alive, it was unlikely they'd encountered this Great Predator before, although they may have come across his barbed contraptions camouflaged in the trees and grass. They may have even lost a member or two to them.

Manno's clan would have been a mix of males and females, some more dominant than others but none more dominant than the patriarch. The patriarch may or may not have been Manno's father, but he would have allowed Manno's mother to feast first amongst the females, if not to ensure the survival of his clan then at least to maintain the alliances that empowered him. But he would have been suspicious of Manno, too; this baby was a male. And a male could grow up to depose the patriarch and take command of the family overnight.

As a child, though, Manno would have spent the majority of his days latched to his mother's front side, riding her upside down until he outgrew that position and piggybacked on her for up to two years. She was his protector and playmate, his feeder and groomer. She would have only put him down to sleep at night.

And that's usually when the Great Predator comes. In packs of two or more. Quiet as can be with long metal strips that chop away the branches and steel barrels that light up with thunderous blasts.

If Manno remembered anything it would be *that*, followed by the shrieking of his family members, all at once. One shrill chimpanzee on its own is deafening, but ten at once would probably have stunned Manno into a paralytic state. Another round of blasts. Branches break and tumble to the ground with 130-pound sacks of flesh. The

shrieking is lessening, but those still able to call do it in long, drawn out screams. Then one final blast and it's quiet. For a few brief moments, the jungle is still.

Manno is trembling, eyes rolling from side to side, his infant mind trying to grasp the carnage and make out his mother from all the bodies, all the mounds of coarse hair still as stone. Branches snap as the predators approach with soft, puttering voices that defy their bloodlust. Manno is scooped up. Whether because he's confused or petrified, he latches onto the body of this tall, lanky ape. Still, he knows it's an outsider from the smell, the smooth and flat fur, and the barbarism that follows.

Using those long steel blades, the predators hack off the heads of his mother, brothers and sisters, and the once fearsome leader, now reduced to pieces. The arms, legs, and torso are bushmeat that might make its way to Europe through a variety of traders, where it'll be consumed as a delicacy. But it's more likely the predators' families will feast on it for the week. The heads, hands, and feet are simply souvenirs of their hunt. The real prize is Manno.

He is, in fact, the entire reason for this slaughter. The cost of a living baby chimp—and the lives of its entire family—is about $50, more than six weeks of wages in the Democratic Republic of the Congo. That poacher will easily find a middleman willing to pay that. What he may not know is for how much Manno might sell next to a well-connected animal trafficker—about $400, almost a year's income.

That new middleman, usually in a major city, will seek a buyer willing to pay upward of $10,000 and who will, in turn, sell Manno to Ramadan for more still. The Congolese dealer, if he doesn't have a buyer already, will have prospects all over the Arab Gulf states, China, and Southeast Asia. He'll be cautious to avoid traps set by Interpol, investigative journalists, or animal rights groups, but he's probably done this dozens, if not hundreds, of times before; he might even have someone on the inside to bypass international controls like CITES, the Convention on International Trade in Endangered Species of

Wild Fauna and Flora. He might be bold enough to sell Manno on Facebook, Snapchat, or Instagram—the latter the favorite amongst exotic animal traders. Those deals over the internet usually come later, though, fetching up to $65,000 for a baby chimp.

Manno, however, is headed for the Mediterranean. His bottom is wrapped in a diaper, and he's placed in a crate that has barely enough space for him to turn his head. He's given a few bananas, and then the compartment is strategically placed on the truck or boat—around it are other crates that house decriminalized and less endangered animals, all of which are viewable through slots. It's important the dealer place a nonendangered monkey or two amongst them to mask Manno's cries and to fool border and permit controllers. Manno's crate probably doesn't get on a plane until it reaches Cairo, crossing through Uganda and Sudan to get there, although that part—like the entire trade and most of what will follow until he lands in Syria—is a mystery. Eventually, Manno is put up for final sale—his price probably marked up another 50 percent by the final seller. Before he arrives at Duhok Zoo, Manno will have changed hands five or six times. Ironically, it's only the last of these transfers that wasn't illegal. Iraq was not a signatory to CITES, and Iraqi law allowed the acquisition and display of a chimp like Manno.

A lot of this is guesswork. A lot of this is extrapolating from countless similar cases of great apes captured, bought, sold, and resold around the world. The only thing we can know for sure is that, if Manno was born in the Congo, then his entire family was slaughtered for our entertainment. Because that's the only way to capture a baby chimpanzee in the wild. There is no other way.

I wished Manno and his zoo-mates had arrived in Duhok the way I did, on the wings of freedom, instead of in the crates of captivity. But my own story of how I first started trying to give back to the world started with a tragedy.

On August 29, 2007, a clear and sunny morning and the first day back to school, I entered the school halls and immediately detected that something was wrong. The first day back is usually marked with excitement for teachers, geared up and happy to see our students and ready to return to our productive modes. Instead, a small group of my colleagues spoke to each other in the halls with hushed tones, unable to look at each other.

"What's going on?" I asked one of them.

"Dan Redeker's daughter died," she said.

Dan and I went back decades, to the first school that hired me. Dan was somewhat of a mentor to me, even if he didn't know it. He was always quick to calm my nerves when the cocky jock in me wanted to fight the latest memorandum to land in our inboxes. "Pick your battles, Spencer," he'd say, always with the same patient demeanor. His smile was a permanent feature, his benevolence unflappable in the face of any high school antics, and though I'd never met his daughter, Melissa, I could tell from the eulogy a couple of days later that she'd inherited the best parts of him.

The number of people who came to pay their respects was so big that I had to park along the highway and walk to the funeral home two hundred meters away. Four or five hundred guests packed the chapel, filling the green pews all the way to the back. I stood in the doorway, waiting for the service to begin.

"It's been a challenge for us to condense a life that was lived so fully, with so much zest, but we will try," a relative said, reading Dan and Diane Redeker's eulogy because the parents were too distraught. "Her curiosity with the world began early with her ferocious love of books. How many of you have read six books at one time?"

The relative continued to paint a picture of the ambitious young woman who leapt into service whenever she was needed and never turned down an adventure. At twenty-one, she was more traveled than most people I knew and had an insatiable desire to do good in the world. On her own, she'd befriended Canadian soldiers overseas

and filled one hundred shoeboxes with toys, clothes, and stationery to send to children affected by the Afghan war. She'd sponsored a child from Malawi through World Vision. She saw these good acts as a starting point to her ultimate goal of volunteering with Doctors Without Borders in Central Africa, to help children infected with AIDS or orphaned by it. She'd started the paramedic training she hoped would take her there but never got to finish her plans. Without warning, a blood clot had formed in her respiratory system and killed her.

"To Melissa," said the speaker, "every dog, every cat, every horse, every person was worthy of her love, attention, and affection. She gave herself one hundred percent to everyone."

I choked back the tears brought on by the compassion of a stranger I'd never had the privilege of knowing. It was inspiring to me to learn how wholeheartedly Melissa had pursued her passions and how selfless those passions were. I was twice her age and yet it had never occurred to me that you could experience nations by volunteering with a charity group there.

For days, I talked about this idea of "voluntourism" with Christie as if she'd never heard of it; it was me who was foreign to it. At some point, she just said what I was afraid to utter myself: "Why don't you go?"

"Go where?" I said.

"Africa. Or anywhere. Volunteer at a school or something." This is why I love Christie. She truly brings out the best in me and has given me the freedom to explore and become who I am today.

Until that point, teaching about people I hadn't met firsthand had felt like being an English instructor teaching a book he hadn't read. I typed "volunteer in Africa" into Google and got a dizzying number of results. I amended it with "teaching," and it was still overwhelming.

I slowly spun in my chair, running through the places I'd taught about and current events that had gripped my students. Suddenly, Sierra Leone popped into my head.

I'd done some research on Sierra Leone when I was preparing my lessons, and what I'd learned had shocked me. The West African nation was still dealing with the aftereffects of a heinous civil war that pitted neighbor against neighbor. The human rights violations were staggering, and Sierra Leone was now in a years-long process of forgiveness. Up to 300,000 people had been killed. There were also hundreds of thousands of reported rapes, an ancient weapon of war, and tens of thousands of limb amputations that had been used not just to intimidate people, but to hinder voting and mining. The country's rich diamond reserves had been used to trade with other nations for weapons, leading to the term "blood diamonds." Everyone knew or was someone who'd been brutalized, but everyone also knew or was someone who'd perpetrated the horrors. There was no other way to move on but through a massive act of forgiveness.

I amended my search once more with "Sierra Leone." The United Nations Human Development Index had listed the country as the second least livable nation in the world. There was a slew of NGOs already operating there, covering gaps in services that the government and foreign aid couldn't manage. One of them was Rhema Preparatory School in Thunder Hill, an eastern district of the capital, Freetown, which had been set up by an evangelical ministry at the tail end of the war. I crafted an email stating my interest in volunteering and clicked send.

I would later learn that I wasn't the only person moved into action by Melissa's memory. She also inspired a young woman to take a medical mission in Haiti. In the years to come, 2,500 shoeboxes were filled with Christmas gifts for underprivileged Canadians in her honor; local junior high students pooled their money to buy livestock for an African village, in her memory; thirteen children were sponsored by World Vision, inspired by her; an astronomer would even name a star after her. Melissa herself had donated her corneas posthumously, and now two complete strangers had sight thanks to her.

It brought to my mind the words of B. J. Palmer, the developer of chiropractic: "You never know how something you think, say, or do today will affect the lives of millions tomorrow." I was starting late, but I hoped I could do my part.

On my final night in Duhok, I didn't start my conversation with Christie with my usual panicked "Christie!" but she still sensed it. All week, I'd sent her photos of Manno, and that night, while packing my belongings, I frantically shared with her everything I'd learned about the great ape trade in Central Africa.

"This isn't right," I said. "Something has to change."

"You're not bringing home a chimp."

"You said, 'no dogs.'"

"Spencer."

"He's just a little baby—"

"Spencer."

"I know, I'm not serious about bringing him home. But we need to get him out."

Christie went silent. Nothing surprised her anymore. Once, in Thailand, we were visiting the Royal Palace when a bird fell out of the sky and landed by my foot, flapping around in agony. I picked it up and started giving it mouth-to-mouth, to the embarrassment of Christie and the disgust of everyone around us. Her silence on the phone let my last few words reverberate in my own head so I could hear myself clearly. *We need to get him out. Yes, I understand I can't just adopt him. No, I don't know my options. Yes, I'm willing to find out.*

"I'm not an expert—I can't help you with this," Christie said. "You're going to have to send out some emails."

"You're right," I said, thankful for the encouragement. "I love you."

"I love you, too. Travel safe tomorrow."

Before I went to bed, I opened my laptop and started searching. I collected every relevant email address I could scrape from the internet:

Interpol, the United Nations Office on Drugs and Crime, CITES, the International Primate Protection League, the International Fund for Animal Welfare, the World Wildlife Fund, a watchdog called Zoo-check, Kurdish president Masoud Barzani, as well as various zoos in Canada and around the world. Soon enough, I had a couple dozen email addresses ready, and I began crafting my letter:

I am contacting you about any possible information that may assist me in channelling the information I have to the proper authorities in regards to illegal animal smuggling that I came across. Can you direct me on how I can best help these animals?

I am a Canadian schoolteacher who worked in Iraq for an NGO over Christmas break. I have come into contact with a private zoo in Duhok, Iraq. I believe the curator of the zoo has purchased all of his animals from smugglers: four Siberian tigers, three leopards, two bears, four lions, two wolves and a chimpanzee, Manno, that he purchased for $15,000. Iraq does not comply with CITES.

My question is what can I do to help these animals, especially Manno, who I grew to love deeply. Is there a way we can get these animals in better conditions?

The curator/owner of that zoo was incredibly gracious and hospitable to me. I do not believe him to be an evil or bad man. The cages are cleaned extensively daily, the animals are fed. He has a vet who sees sick or injured animals. He gave me incredible detail on how he brings in the smuggled animals (see photos and price lists attached). In his view he is doing nothing wrong, as he is not breaking any Iraqi/Kurdish laws.

It is especially heart-wrenching for me to know that these animals were all once free.

Please help.
Spencer Sekyer

I started from the top of my address list. Copy, paste, click send. Over and over. I wasn't sure what, if anything, my letters would bring. I knew I was out of my depth. But I could feel it coming on, that force in my gut that said "go with this," and that feeling told me that my life was about to change forever once more.

Early the next morning, I made my way out to Sulaiman's truck in the darkness. My flight wasn't until the late afternoon, but we were leaving early that morning because Sulaiman wanted to show me something "very, very important" in Erbil on my way out.

"You must see the zoo," he said once we were on the road. "I think this, maybe, is the worst zoo in the world—after one I saw in Egypt. After that, this is the worst. It is like jail, Spencer!"

"I don't know if I can take that right now," I said. "I'm already brokenhearted saying goodbye to Manno."

"Now you will meet Manno's brother."

Sulaiman explained to me what Ramadan could not due to language barriers: Manno had not traveled alone. The Duhok Zoo tried to purchase two chimps, a male and a female, but when the cargo arrived at the Syrian border, both were males. They were not actually brothers, but they did come as a pair. Since they couldn't breed, Ramadan only bought Manno. The other found a buyer in Erbil.

"Ramadan said he bought Manno from Baghdad," I said.

"No. Not Baghdad. He drove to Syria by himself and got Manno. He has permits."

"How? Isn't that against international law?"

"Spencer, Iraq has not signed CITES." Sulaiman had seen the official documents required for Manno's transfer stamped by the Ministry of Environment. They'd allowed Ramadan's purchase of the animals from Zakho, a border city near where Iraq, Syria, and Turkey meet. "When the Syria war started, many, many animals had to leave the zoos. They were very, very cheap."

"You think Manno came from a zoo?"

"Maybe—but I will show you." He was being very vague, but I let him keep me in suspense.

As we approached Erbil's Gilkand Zoo, I grew even more confused. The compound was small—maybe one or two thousand square meters—and the inside looked bombed out. Scattered ropes, wires, and steel sheets were everywhere; garbage spread across the grass that camels grazed on; and the floors of the twelve concrete huts housing the animals were littered with junk food wrappers. The entire zoo looked like you could destroy it with a hammer in half a day, and that someone had already started.

"All zoos in Iraq are private sector," Sulaiman said as we climbed the chipped stairs into the main square. "For example, whether you are rich man, you are poor man, if you want to open a zoo you can open one that's one hundred meters. Secondly, it means the government has no role. We have veterinary quarantine, but they know nothing. If you bring in a lion, tiger, elephant, it's the same as if you brought a cat. If it looks healthy, they say, 'Go.' A rich man can even bring in a lion for himself."

"For his home?" I asked.

"*Yez*! Tiger, hyena, cheetah. It is a symbol of a big man."

"You know people—"

"*Yez*. Last week I treated two baby gazelles."

There were no barriers protecting us from the animals in this zoo, and though I'd broken that rule in Duhok (and relearned a valuable lesson), I was concerned for the handful of children in the presence of a lioness with a wounded tail.

She roared at the children from her kennel—at nine feet wide, that's all it was. A wolf nearby had half that space and was jumping off the walls in an effort to expend his energy. Sadness seeped into every part of me as I watched these animals who were slowly going insane. A baboon displayed similar behavior in a space smaller still. A man stood over the baboon, talking to it while he smoked a cigarette. I saw him extend his hand, offering the cigarette to the baboon to eat.

"No," I said. "Don't do that."

He said something in Kurdish, barely acknowledging me.

"Come on, man," I said, growing angrier.

He said something else I couldn't understand, this time looking at me defensively.

I cursed, then my impatience got the better of me, and I blurted, "How about I punch you in the head?" He put the cigarette back between his lips and walked away.

We finished the dreadful tour in minutes. Sulaiman hadn't exaggerated when he called it the world's worst zoo, and it certainly changed my perspective on Ramadan's operation. The Duhok Zoo was clean and vast compared to this.

"Where's the chimp?" I asked.

"He's not here," Sulaiman said.

"You said he went to Erbil."

"He did."

"So where is he?"

"Exactly. Where is Manno's brother?" He paused. "This is not a zoo. This is a pet shop."

I had no words.

"You want to save Manno. Okay, you save Manno. But if you spend money on Manno, fly him to Africa, and give him back to the wild, they will find another Manno. That is business, Spencer."

"Is that what you brought me here to show me? You could have just said so, you know."

"No," Sulaiman said with a smile. "I come here to show you zoo for the last time. I will shut this down. I will show you. No more Erbil Zoo."

2: Lessons from Abroad

WINTER 2014–FALL 2016

Chapter five

"The purpose of life is to live it, to taste experience to the utmost, to reach out eagerly and without fear for newer and richer experience."

—ELEANOR ROOSEVELT

Back in Edmonton, I walked down the escalator to the arrivals terminal, scanning the faces in the baggage area for Christie. When we locked eyes, a rush of joy washed through me. I couldn't get down the escalator fast enough. We embraced at the bottom of the stairs, my nose buried in her neck. Her curly brown hair was still slightly damp from her morning shower, and I breathed in its tropical smell that I'd so dearly missed.

"You get any sleep?" she asked as we walked, arm in arm, to the baggage claim.

"Not much," I said. "I can't stop thinking about my buddy Manno."

"Is there anything you can do to help him?"

"There has to be," I said. "I'm going to find out."

We hauled my bags down to the parking garage. I tossed the bags in the back of the truck and instinctively reached for the handle on the driver's side. It was locked, and I started fishing in my pockets for the keys, patting down my body with a perplexed look.

Christie started laughing. I looked up and she dangled the keys. "Maybe you and your jet lag should stay off the road," she said with a smile.

"Good idea."

I slumped in the passenger seat and stared out the window at the white fields surrounding the airport. I could see across the prairies for miles and miles, near limitless snow reflecting the sun up at me. I shut my eyes to protect them against the overwhelming brightness and fell soundly asleep.

The next thing I saw was the acreage road to our house. The skies were no longer clear blue, though. They were impossible to see behind a suddenly savage blizzard that was scrambling my view like TV static. Christie was beside me, white-knuckled, leaning forward with her chin practically on the wheel, squinting through the blizzard. "Who's that?" she asked.

I looked ahead. Someone was standing at the edge of the road, a lanky figure with outstretched arms. The car felt like it was floating toward the figure, no brakes, let alone the guidance of either legs or tires—just floating on a wind that seemed too smooth for the storm.

The blizzard suddenly blew away, clearing my view, and though I couldn't see the figure's face, I could see the bundle lying perfectly still in its cupped hands. It was a baby, swaddled and obscured. Before I could see the baby closely, though, it began glowing whiter than white, its elastic aura stretching to half the size of the person holding it and then—*PHWOOOOK*—a blast of light filled my vision and the baby disintegrated into millions of effervescent rainbow-colored particles that scattered everywhere.

I awoke with a jolt. Christie and I sat in the truck in our roundabout driveway, and it was even brighter outside than it was in my dream, thanks to the mighty prairie sunshine.

"We're home," Christie said.

I unbuckled myself and leaned in for a kiss.

I pulled my bags from the backseat while Christie opened the door to the garage. Chloe and Mac, yowling like Wookies, ambushed me and I fell on my backside. Their bodies wriggled uncontrollably, snaking around my legs with their ears pinned down out of joy. Burying

my face into their necks, I spoke in a voice that only Christie and dogs were ever allowed to hear: "Oh my little muffins, how I missed you, too. Yes, yes, daddy's home. I love you, too."

I'd thought about my dogs constantly while I was away—Chloe, Mac, and Emma (who stayed with our neighbor and dog trainer friend most days to protect her from Chloe's wrathful jealousy). The surge of excitement was mutual, although Mac was especially over-the-top. He shook like a rocket about to launch, and his left eye, always slightly off-kilter, looked in the other direction as he struggled to contain himself. Chloe, in her old age, was more lethargic—she was now deaf as a stone and had the vision of a month-old puppy. She compensated by aggressively sniffing me, as if triple-checking to verify I wasn't an imposter. I could imagine no better homecoming than the one I got from Christie and our dogs. I kissed the smooth groove between each of the dogs' eyes, threw my arms around their necks, and cooed to them—essentially, I did everything that dog behavioralists tell you not to do.

I woke up the next morning the same way I always did: with a shot of apple cider vinegar. After the intensity of the vinegar opened my throat, I washed down an assortment of supplements, drops, oils, and vitamins—each one awakening me another degree—and stepped barefoot into the frigid, black morning.

I flipped the vinyl lid halfway off the hot tub and submerged myself in the bubbling tank. My head tilted toward the moon suspended in the inky sky, tasting the coolness of the snowflakes tumbling onto my tongue. The hot and cold cranked my eyes open wider as I adjusted to the darkness. The gurgling bubbles reminded me of the cute sounds Manno made when he drank from his bottle. I wondered if he was thinking about me, too. *Are chimpanzees able to miss their human caretakers?* I wondered. *When we leave them in their cages and crates overnight, do they wonder what we're doing in our cages and crates?*

I wondered if Manno thought about me as much as I thought

about him, or if he saw me as just another hairless ape with long arms he could jump in and out of. I wished he knew that, as happy as I was to be home, I was sad to be away from him. What would become of my new friend? Or had he already become an old friend?

My body clenched as I climbed out of the water and tiptoed across the frost. Back inside, I shaved and dressed, pulling the blanket over Christie's shoulder before heading downstairs to start my day.

After working out, I sat at my computer and opened my email, hoping for better news about Manno than what I'd been getting. It had only been a couple of days since I'd left Kurdistan, but a number of the NGOs, state departments, and zoos I'd written to had already replied. Each of them had the same thing to say: "Sorry." At best, they referred me to another agency that gave another version of the same apology.

Each of the animal rights groups would have loved to see Manno in a sanctuary—the wild was not an option for an orphan chimp, as he'd never be able to survive on his own. But Manno was just one thread in a cloak of secrecy obscuring something much bigger than him: the multibillion-dollar trade of illegal apes. Without solid information about the exact smugglers or routes that had taken Manno from his home—I couldn't even square what Ramadan had told me with what he'd apparently told Sulaiman—there wasn't anything the major organizations I was contacting could do.

I reread the old emails and flagged the new ones worth a reply, then started dressing for work. But as I quietly pulled a shirt off the hanger, careful not to wake Christie, I had a feeling in my stomach that something about my home routine today was off. *Did I forget something?* No, something forgot me. It was Mac. Where was he?

Mac was usually my shadow from the first minute of the morning to my last seconds of wakefulness. He curled up and slept at the foot of my side of the bed, then pressed his cold nose against my cheek when it was time to start my day, usually around 5:00 a.m. My pupils would roll into place and see his cockeyed stare, saying *oh, hi* to me, his

gaze never wavering until I was on my feet. I should have heard him pitter-patter up the stairs after I got up, and I should have heard him scratching at the closed office door like Freddy Krueger. But I didn't.

I looked down at the spot by our bed where Mac slept. It was empty. I scanned the corners of the room and searched the rest of the house to no avail. I found Chloe sleeping in her spot—the front door-mat, where the cool breeze from the crack under the door soothed her—but there was no sign of Mac.

I checked the doggy door leading outside into our backyard. We had a fence, but Mac was quite the escape artist. *It's way too cold and dark for Mac to go off frolicking on his own, right?* My stomach tensed at the thought that I could be wrong.

There were paw prints in the fresh snow outside the door flap. I followed them into the bush until the gray streaks in Mac's fur revealed him in the dark. I rushed over and found him curled up in a patch of tall brown grass under a small spruce tree. He blinked at me with droopy eyes. "You okay, buddy?" I asked, scratching under his chin. I lifted him to his feet and he walked back to the house on his own, slipping back inside through the doggy door. He seemed okay, but I was worried. Mac's behavior had never changed in thirteen years. For him to act so differently the morning after I returned home told me one thing: something was wrong.

I took one more look at the acreage, then walked past our bee-hives back toward the house. I followed Mac inside and tried to put the scare behind me. I grabbed my laptop and drove to school, ready to greet my students. I already knew how I was going to open the first class back—I'd prepared a presentation about Kurdish people and the right to self-determination, as always trying to turn some of what I'd learned firsthand into classroom lectures that fit the curriculum.

I was quick to adapt to my work routine after a long break, connecting my computer to the projector, organizing my teaching notes, greeting my colleagues through the doorway and students as they trickled in.

"Everybody say *shhhhhhh*," I said with a finger to my lips. By that point, my students knew the drill. They silenced each other and I was able to welcome them back from Christmas break.

"How was Iraq?" asked Vanessa, leaning forward.

"You survived!" said Jonathan from the very back.

"Mr. Sekyer was in Iraq?" asked one of the girls.

"Were you fighting terrorists?" a boy asked all too sincerely, earning unwanted chuckles from the room. Another kid lifted his arms in front like he was handling an invisible machine gun and flapped his lips to imitate firing. "Yeah, Seeks!" he said.

"No, he's a spy!" quipped another.

"Not quite," I said. "Actually, I was pretty safe where I was." I told them what I'd been doing there and how I came to meet Manno, and a debate started immediately.

"Aren't there, like, people dying there?" asked Vanessa.

"Yeah, who cares about a monkey?" said Jonathan.

"Ape," I corrected him. "Chimps are apes. Primates like us, but I get where you're coming from. There are lots of refugees there who could benefit from my charity, right? Kids who deserve a better education I could help. People who want to get out of there, get a better life. So, yeah, who cares about an animal?"

"Or why not help animals here?" asked Carly. "Instead of letting them get euthanized."

"Or that," I said.

"What about people?" Vanessa stressed again. "There are so many homeless in Canada. Thousands."

"A lot of hungry people," Liam added.

"Fair point," I admitted. "But where does it end? There are lots of causes that need money, volunteers, advocates, but it's much easier to cop out of them by saying, 'What about this, or what about that?' There will always be someone or something in greater need. But here's the difference: that chimpanzee in Iraq was in front of me and, you know when you see something that you know isn't right, and

you think, 'Someone should do something about that'? Well, why is it always someone else? And at the end of the day, we're all someone."

What I didn't admit to them was that this was way out of my depth. I'd dabbled in animal rescue before—I'd helped transfer deer from the local rehab center, found homes for sick and stray dogs both locally and thousands of miles away. But I had never done something as complex and involved as rescuing a primate, let alone one obtained through the black market. But I kept this to myself and listened to my young critics.

"I just think that if you're in Canada, you should help Canadian animals," said Vanessa.

Those were the moments I savored, when I could cease to be an educator and instead be a mediator, allowing for the students' critical faculties to steer the conversation.

It was good to be back and sink into the comfort of my classroom, but I couldn't help feel some unrest growing inside me. Nothing had changed in my environment, yet I felt significantly different. It was something I'd experienced intensely once before, back in 2008. That was the year I embarked on my first solo voluntourism trip, to Sierra Leone.

The terrible evidence of Sierra Leone's civil war was immediate and stark, sitting before my eyes as soon as I arrived at Lungi International Airport and on the ferry ride to the country's capital, Freetown. No matter how impolite it was, I found it impossible to look away from the stumps protruding from shirtsleeves and tank tops, or hiding under sagging pant legs tied in a knot around the knee. Each person's injury took on unique characteristics in its healing. The flesh of a young man's elbows was scaly and charcoal colored. An older woman in the crowd caught me looking at her knob of a wrist, the whitened flesh folding in on itself. I assumed they were a few of the tens of thousands of victims of the Revolutionary United Front (RUF) rebels

who turned the government's slogan, "The future is in your hands," into a cruel joke when they hacked off people's hands and limbs to keep them from picking up guns to fight back, pens to vote, or tools to mine the nation's precious diamonds.

Feeling rude, I turned to look out at the approaching Freetown coast. Below me, a crush of people shuffled toward the open bow as it approached Kissy Ferry Terminal at the foot of long green hills almost as bright as the head wraps and dresses the women around me wore.

Passengers hustled off the ferry before it came to a full stop, and darted up the hill, presumably to guarantee a bus seat. I made my way downstairs and was shuffling through the crowd when I felt a body slam into my left shoulder. I turned to see a young man hastily forcing himself through the bodies. I instinctively tapped the large pocket in my cargo shorts where I kept my camera—empty!

I was about to panic, but then I felt a tap on my shoulder. It was a woman with a baby cradled in a sarong over her back. "*Tifman*," she said, pointing to a different guy on my right.

The man she pointed at was quickly pushing his way through the crowd to get away. I grabbed him by the shirt collar, and he immediately presented my digital camera laying flat on his palm, surrendering it without a fight. I snatched it back with one hand and paused. What did one do in a situation like that? Bring him to the police—what police? Make a citizen's arrest?

I swore and let the man go. I flipped my backpack around to my chest and put the camera away; a zippered pocket had already been tampered with by someone trying to snag what was inside.

That was my introduction to Sierra Leone. My heart was still racing when I finally disembarked the ferry ten minutes later. I was on the lookout for a man named Francis Kamara—a dead ringer for Wesley Snipes, judging from the photo he emailed me—but he picked me out of the crowd first.

"Spensa!"

Francis, wearing a baggy white long-sleeve shirt, introduced me

to his son, Woodie—real name Abraham—who helped his pastor father and teacher mother run Rhema Preparatory School, where I'd be teaching for the summer.

"Ow di bodi?" asked Woodie as we shook hands. I assumed from his upward inflection that this was a question.

"Sorry?" I replied.

"Di bodi, di bodi," he repeated. "How nah Spensa?"

I was light-headed. One of the reasons I'd thought Sierra Leone would be easier to navigate was because English was supposedly its official language, but I was quickly learning that most people spoke a creole, or Krio—the word itself a type of creole—and I realized I could barely decipher a word it. Not only was I supposed to be a self-sufficient guest, but I was somehow expected to teach middle schoolers, despite the language barrier. That wasn't all that overwhelmed me, either. Nothing felt remotely familiar, neither the thick, damp, hot July air, nor the smell of saltwater infused with petrol and burning charcoal. Scads of skinny stray dogs and chickens roamed the wet, red earth, amongst the sandals attached to sweaty guys pushing trailer carts and ladies with basket loads balanced atop their heads. People shared the streets with zooming motorcycle taxis and dented vans that doubled as buses, each with hand-painted slogans like "Give your heart to God" on the flat-nosed front.

In retrospect, it was perhaps too stimulating for my first solo trip. The terror must have been apparent on my face because Francis just started laughing. "He asks, 'How are you?'" explained Francis. "*How's the body?*"

"The body is good, I guess."

"We will have to teach you Krio," he said through a grin that immediately soothed my nerves.

The Kamaras lived humbly, but they were better off than most Sierra Leoneans. They resided in a long cement house painted in a single, blotchy coat of white and gray that was scaling off. It would have been a decent size for just the couple and their son, Woodie, but it

also housed Ruth, their housekeeper, and four orphans of war. Esther, Betty, and brothers Gabriel and Moses came from separate families destroyed by the rebel factions vying for Freetown. The Kamaras had originally taken in the four children when they were students, just trying to give them a stable environment, but they were now part of the family. Likewise, Ruth was every bit a part of the clan, though her stay was temporary, just until she could find employment as a caterer. In exchange for room and board, she kept the busy house in order.

The entire month I was there, Ruth never left her feet. The airline had lost my luggage, and until it arrived many days later, she cleaned my only two shirts daily on a washboard and ironed them with an ancient-looking iron filled with coals heated outside in a clay pit. The pit was also where my big bucket of shower water was heated every morning. As she did her duties, Ruth taught me about Sierra Leone and told me about the day she'd thought she'd die.

In the early hours of January 6, 1999, a day that lives in infamy as the Invasion of Freetown, the RUF made a second and last attempt at seizing the capital city. Ruth was rounded up with thousands of civilians and coerced to follow the rebels through the smoking, jammed streets to the State House under the pretense that they wanted peace. "All that we were supposed to do was to join their chanting of 'We want peace, we want peace,'" said Ruth, speaking with the Krio blend of formal and colloquial English. "But it was clear to us that the RUF were having an ulterior motive." She suspected the rebels wanted to punish civilians for rejecting them and driving them out of the capital a year prior, and for supporting an international intervention that had ended the RUF's brief reign. Even at fourteen, Ruth understood that the RUF wanted vengeance, and she knew she could be raped or murdered or both by soldiers as young as eight—themselves coerced into brutality.

"On our way going, I stayed behind and escaped alone to a building which was a relaxation bar," she continued. "There I met other people who were also trying to protect their lives."

I sat at the edge of my desk chair, listening intently as she recounted the next hour in her story.

"We were so many that one cannot differentiate between the rebels. Nobody was saying anything, not until another group of RUF arrived with continuous shooting and then they identify themselves and told us to keep calm. A man was trying to escape, then the rebels shoot him as a warning to us.

"I told one of them that I wanted to ease myself," she said. "He told me do it in front of them. But fortunately for me, one of the RUF allowed me to find a suitable place. That was perfect opportunity for me." Ruth snuck away through the bathroom window. She lost track of the days spent hiding in an open-air market in central Freetown, while buildings in the distance were decimated by flames, and cries for help filled the air. Those were amongst the final days of the war. The most heinous days, characterized by summary executions of about five thousand people, and many more rapes, mutilations, and permanent displacements.

I was rapt as she told her story, and I would soon understand that it was a common one. I wondered how a society so traumatized by barbarism, and still suffering for it, could ever trust each other again and build unity. But somehow they did. Sierra Leoneans never cease to amaze me.

Throughout the year, I often told stories like that to animate the foreign lands my students had read about, to humanize real people living there, to help my students see, smell, and hear the land by walking in my shoes.

Perspective was something I was learning much about since returning from Kurdistan. In the week since finding Mac alone outside, he'd only turned more inward and more lethargic. Christie and I became increasingly concerned. After carrying him in my arms from the back of the truck into a vet clinic for a blood test, we received devastating news: Mac had kidney failure.

I had never thought Chloe might outlive Mac. In the last few years, it had been one health issue after another with her. Last fall, around the time I'd booked my trip to Kurdistan, she had collapsed in the hallway. I'd called Christie, telling her, "I think this is it. I think we're going to have to put her down tomorrow." But, when the next day came, there Chloe was, sitting at the front door, bright as ever.

Every day after the diagnosis, as Mac's food and water intake diminished, we carried him to our bed and stuck an IV needle between his shoulder blades to hydrate him and keep his kidneys from failing. Sometimes, he'd whimper and we'd feel helpless—the medication only did so much to alleviate his pain.

I took all of my pain and sadness and tried to channel it into something positive. If I couldn't save Mac, I could still at least still try to save Manno.

After being ignored by virtually everyone I contacted, I received a hopeful message from a woman from the United Kingdom representing an animal-rights group. The group claimed to have recently helped move animals from Kurdistan to a sanctuary, and they were willing to do the same for Manno.

When I first received the woman's email, adrenaline pulsed through me. But the more we spoke, the more my spirits dampened. It turned out the woman's experts were psychics and astrologers. Her intentions were sincere, but I just couldn't take them seriously. Still, my politeness genes, a Canadian inheritance, wouldn't allow me to cut communications, and she continued to send me positive encouragement.

Eventually, I did make one big break: a friend in Afghanistan put me in touch with Cheryl Bernard, an American author, researcher, cultural preservationist, and nature conservationist. She also happened to be married to the former US ambassador to Iraq and was a personal friend of Kurdish prime minister Nechirvan Idris Barzani.

Prompted by a tour of some of Iraq's worst zoos, Cheryl had written a report on animal welfare in Kurdistan, hoping to influence

policy there. In 2012, she helped advocate for the release of Bozo, a Syrian brown bear chained up and for sale at a pet store in Iraqi Kurdistan, and she offered some advice for my campaign for Manno: be patient and persistent.

Cheryl tried to explain the world I was entering.

"It's a lot like the situation in Europe two hundred years ago," she explained in an email, "where monarchs and other aristocrats used to give each other gifts of exotic animals. This is still done in Kurdistan." She shared a shocking anecdote she'd heard from the wife of a leading politician, who'd told Cheryl that dinner guests sometimes brought her an exotic animal the way we might bring a friend a bottle of wine. "She doesn't know what to do with them and gives them to one of the zoos."

I was beginning to understand why the animals in zoos were treated with such little value. A businessperson who spent tens of thousands of dollars on attractions would want to get the most of them and maintain them as you might an expensive and precious instrument. But there was little incentive to do so when wealthy people were dumping animals on you.

As I went to bed that night, my mind teemed as I tried to digest Mac's worsening condition and the news that rescuing Manno was going to be more complicated than I'd thought. When I finally fell asleep, my dreams were unlike any other I'd ever had.

I looked down and there was a stranger by my side. A boy with blond hair limping through the snow. He looked up at me with steel-blue eyes, chubby cheeks, and porcelain skin, and I instantly knew that he was my son.

My heart fluttered as he smiled at me.

We joined hands, just us two, and I noticed that, in addition to his limp, he was wearing a huge studded belt. It was a gaudy thing around his waist—something a glam metal singer from the 1980s might wear—and as we walked up to a brick school, I thought, *Oh, little guy. You're going to get teased so badly for that.* He giggled, opening up a fire hose of joy that blasted through me. The purest love I'd ever felt.

I woke up smiling, eyes fixed to the bedroom ceiling, parsing my emotions as I listened to Christie's soft, unconscious breaths and Mac's whistling snores below me.

I put a lot of stock in my dreams, the key holder to the subconscious, and this was the second sign in a short time nudging me into doing something I never thought I'd want to do.

Christie and I lived fulfilling, independent lives full of adventure, travel, and volunteerism, and we were dedicated to our careers. We never felt like we were missing out on anything. And yet . . .

"Christie," I whispered. "Christie." I nudged her shoulders until she rolled toward me with her eyes closed.

"What?"

"We have to have a baby."

Her eyelids snapped open. She stared at me, unsure if she was the one dreaming now. I repeated what I'd just said.

"Who are you and what did you do to my husband?" she asked.

Chapter six

"The greatness of a nation and its moral progress can
be judged by the way its animals are treated."

—MAHATMA GANDHI

The last few months of the winter in 2014 were bittersweet. After having Mac by my side almost every day for a quarter of my life, I wasn't ready to lose him. I was desperate to keep him alive. But despite daily intravenous fluid sessions, his kidneys continued to fail, and the likelihood of him recovering was slipping from his paws.

"You'll be okay," I told him, as I lay with him on the area rug in the living room, running my hands across his snout and head.

Christie watched from the top of the stairs. She draped her jacket over the side of the couch, put her purse down, and joined me on the floor. "How are my boys?" she said, scratching behind Mac's ears.

"I'm not sure we can bring him back," I whispered, as if Mac might hear me and get scared.

"We can try," she said.

"What if that's just making him suffer more? I don't know if we're doing the right thing by keeping him alive."

She put her hand on my mine. "He'd let us know if this were hurting him. He's a smart boy."

I rolled onto my back and looked at her, feeling so grateful to have such a calm and reassuring soul mate. I touched her belly. "How's our other boy?"

"Or girl," she said.

"It's a boy."

She laughed. "Didn't you once dream that a succubus tried to take your soul while you were paralyzed in bed?"

"It did!"

"Never say never."

Until that point, Christie and I had felt like we had all the family we needed. We had each other, we had the dogs, and in many ways, Christie's practice was her baby. We didn't feel like we were missing out on anything. We understood that if we had a baby, Christie would have to take her hands off the wheel of her business for some time, something she'd never done before in her twenty-year career, but she wouldn't have to step away for too long if I got parental leave.

Still, Christie and I traveled frequently, sometimes alone, but usually together like a duo on *The Amazing Race*—packing a month's worth of adventure into very little time. Christie was the cautious planner, and I was the free spirit always trying to just wing it.

Since I'd started my voluntourism, Christie and I often planned our trips around wherever I'd secured a volunteer spot, tacking on a bit of vacation at the beginning or end of my work. One of the most memorable trips we took was when she came to meet me in Tel Aviv at the end of my contract volunteer teaching at a school in a West Bank refugee camp. I'd been there for a month but hadn't crossed the Green Line into Israel since the start of my placement. I picked up Christie from Ben Gurion Airport in a rental car, we stayed a night in a hotel, and the next morning, we returned to the refugee camp in Bethlehem so she could meet my students and new friends. The next day, we headed back to Jerusalem, navigating checkpoints and getting lost on the city's cramped, mountainous roads, ending up in all the wrong areas.

The highlight, though, was our trip to the Dead Sea one night under a full moon. It was a surreal experience, the desert hills appearing almost like the moonscape itself. As I floated under the night

sky in the warm, thick water, Christie warned, "Do not put your face underwater."

"It's fine if I close my eyes," I said, dipping my head back. As my ears came back to the surface, I heard a lady wading in the sea beside us scolding me in Russian. I tried to open my eyes and groaned in pain at the salt water stinging them. My eyes clenched tightly, she and Christie had to guide me back to shore for a shower to rinse off.

We didn't slow down after that. The next day, we were in Petra, Jordan, and then we circled back, through Aqaba and its 45°C heat, to Tel Aviv, and then through Egypt, before flying back home.

As I recalled those memorable few days, I tried to run them back and replay them with a baby or kid by our side.

At the same time, we'd met so many fellow travelers across the globe who sojourned with small children—albeit at a much slower pace—and their families always seemed better for it. In fact, Christie had a trip planned to Rwanda for the day after my birthday, just a few months away. She planned to volunteer with a chiropractor friend in youth prisons, doing adjustments for children, most of them from the country's poorest areas. She wasn't about to set that aside. If we did have a kid, we wanted to show our new family member the world from their very first moments.

I still recall how vivid our boy had seemed in my dream, and how absolutely joyous it left me for days after. I felt it again whenever I rubbed Christie's belly and sang to him.

But it was hard to hold on to that feeling when I heard Mac whimpering in the corner of our living room. How we treat our animals is a measure of something about our societies. Stability, maybe. A measure of basic welfare, the luxury of focusing on our animal friends instead of our human ones, perhaps. From what I'd seen, if people within a society weren't having their needs met, then animal protections fell a long way down the priority list.

Thinking back to my time in Sierra Leone, I vividly recalled its most desperate parts. Ramshackle stores and homes that looked as if

they'd been thrown together with spare wood, corrugated aluminum, and cardboard. Families crouched around firepits in dirt floors. Outside, children climbed what looked like open landfills. And it seemed on every corner there were victims of war begging for money or food with containers between their stumps.

The human struggle was vivid and widespread, and the conditions of the animals mirrored those of the people around them. Without a spay-and-neuter program, thousands of feral dogs roamed the streets, fighting for scraps and cowering from abusers. Shopkeepers threw rocks at strays to keep them from their produce; kids copied the adults, sometimes hurling stones just for fun. Yelps that I seldom heard at home were almost constantly audible if I strained my ears enough.

And yet, despite the suffering and pain that people had suffered, there was still compassion to be found. And in my time there, I was fortunate to witness it firsthand at Tacugama, the chimp sanctuary that sparked my initial interest in great apes.

A cab driver took me to the Western Area Forest Reserve south of Freetown, weaving his car down the red earth road and around giant potholes pooling with water. We were headed toward the verdant jungle hillsides, the fields around us slowly transforming into the lush jungle of the highlands. Every so often, he had to stop and reverse to allow oncoming cars to pass, complaining in Krio the entire time as if it were my fault. By the time we arrived, the car windows and my camera lens were foggy from the humidity.

I stepped out into the pouring rain and entered through the gates. At first glance, the park looked much cleaner and better organized than any place in Sierra Leone I'd seen, but that was only the first of my expectations shattered by the experience.

At the time, I was still naïve—I thought it would be wonderful to have a pet chimpanzee like you saw in movies. Chimps seemed so human and friendly, and I didn't yet know enough to think otherwise. The instant I entered Tacugama, though, that fantasy vanished. The

first thing the guide showed me was the chimps' "play area." The apes screamed and kicked each other while swinging from ropes, dropping their playmates from dangerously tall heights. It was like watching one violent NFL football hit after another. *This is their play?* I thought. It looked more like chimpanzee fight club.

A short time later, I walked down to a section of the jungle where a group of chimpanzees were sitting near the electrified wires.

"Be careful," warned the guide. "They will throw rocks at you."

I was mesmerized by the apes, though. It was my first encounter with them so close. So, naturally, I wandered too close to the fence. A chimpanzee near the front grabbed a red rock the size of a grapefruit and lobbed it underhand at me. It landed a few meters from me. Was this a warning? I couldn't help but laugh at its attempt to assault me.

Suddenly, two other chimps lobbed rocks at me, each landing closer, and within seconds, it was raining rocks around me. I tried to fend off the onslaught with my elbows as the animals shrieked with victory.

My guide later told me about the troop's former alpha male, Bruno, who had staged a recent escape that tragically led to Bruno killing a man. And yet, the guide told me, when the RUF had attempted a hostile takeover of the national park, they had spared the Tacugama caretakers' lives and left them to take care of the chimps.

Every experience during that trip shaped my view of the world in new ways. One day, as I sat in my room in the Kamaras' home, Ruth brought me two small grilled herrings—head still on—on a plate of plain noodles for lunch. She left me alone to eat at my desk in the family's Spartan, single-room guesthouse. A scrawny cat wandered through the open door and rubbed its head against my legs. When I was finished eating, I put the plate of fish bones on the floor for it. Francis came by to check on me and immediately disapproved.

"Spencer," he said, lifting the plate off the floor and shooing away the cat, "it might not be so good to do that." He asked me not to feed the animals anymore. I assumed it was to keep them from becoming

a nuisance. But a little later, on my way to the outhouse, I saw the family's two adopted girls squatting over my plate outside, sucking the meat flakes off my fish bones. I had always been conscious of eating what was on my plate—a maxim drilled into me as a child—but in that moment, I realized that waste was all a matter of perspective.

The Kamaras' school, Rhema Preparatory School, reminded me of a discarded building in an industrial district. Back home, it would be hardly noticeable but for the bright blue trimming leaping off the blotchy white exterior. As I followed Francis up the concrete steps to the second floor, where the secondary students had their single classroom, I heard a crack and a bloodcurdling scream.

Inside, a boy was bent forward with his palms flat atop a wooden desk. A teacher stood behind him with a long willow branch. The rest of the children watched on, either giggling or tensed up knowing they could be next. The switch cracked him a second time and I winced.

"Is something wrong?" Francis asked.

What was going through my mind was: *If I did that as a teacher, not only would I be fired but it'd make the front page of the local newspaper.* What came out of my mouth was: nothing. It was my first time in any sort of situation like that where I was the outsider looking in, but I wasn't about to impose my values, so I kept quiet. And anyway, the attention had quickly turned to me. Even the boy against the wall stared at me with his head tilted while he massaged his butt.

"Whitaman! Whitaman!" the children shouted, pushing away from the communal desks and charging for me like I was a rock star. They tugged at my hands and shirt, hugging my legs, literally tearing the blond hair off my arms. I knelt down to be at their eye level and felt little arms and legs climbing onto my back. I could barely get a word in between laughing. I let the kids have their fun, until Francis called an end to it. He promised them I'd be back after we finished the tour.

Francis and his wife, Mariatu, started Rhema as both a school and a church in 2000, fifteen years after they met on a United Methodist

Church mission, and a year after Francis had returned from Nigeria with his theology degree. "At the end of my course, I returned home and shared the vision for the school with Mariatu," he said as we walked around the schoolyard, my shoes turning red as they trounced the dirt. "She said, 'Francis, this is our destiny. I also received the vision.'"

Francis relayed that same vision to me, speaking with a formality that made me self-conscious of my own English. "Our desire was to provide basic educational facilities for children affected by the war, in order to build them up into responsible citizens." The school had two hundred primary students but only thirty-five in junior high because, by their late teens, many Sierra Leoneans were expected to exit school and find work to help support their families. "The war dealt us a savage blow. Amongst other things, it destroyed socioeconomic development and battered the educational system, leaving behind a lot of children forced to go out to the street to beg or do odd jobs for a living."

"Esther, Betty, and the brothers?" I asked.

He nodded. "We found Gabriel and Moses in the Freetown market, sleeping on tables beside fish. They lost their parents when the rebels entered the city. Esther's parents were buried alive in a water well by the Kamajor rebels. And Betty, her mother couldn't look after her alone, so she brought her to our church and we adopted her. There have been other children, too, and some of them have gone to live for themselves, gone to universities, living abroad. We hope that the children reach their God-given potentials."

"I'll do my best to help," I said.

A strain of laughter suddenly exploded from the building as barefooted children broke for recess. My eyes followed a group of boys who darted past Francis and me, eager to reach the edge of the school grounds, where there appeared to be nothing but a shallow trench. They started undoing their pants and squatting, and I immediately averted my eyes when I realized they were going to the bathroom.

I hurried to catch up with Francis. He led me back inside to my

classroom on the upper level where I'd be teaching social studies—teaching junior high students about Sierra Leone, students who no doubt knew far more about the country than me. As I stepped inside, I wondered who would be learning the most, them or me?

The classroom was one giant room with low ceilings, separated into four areas. Each space had a small, broken, square blackboard, smeared with layers of white chalk dust, and a cluster of sturdy wooden communal desks and pews that gave it an air of church. The children ambushed me again after they returned from recess. I felt them pulling at the blond hair on my arms. I yelped and laughed, struggling to free my limbs. It took some wrangling, but I eventually got them to sit in their desks.

I'd been preparing the curriculum for some time, but I'd also spent the past weekend trying to learn Krio basics—*wetin nah u name?* ("what's your name?") and *wetin u go nid?* ("what will you need?"), as well as the all-encompassing Sierra Leonean greeting, "*How da bodi?*" It turned out I wouldn't need it—Mariatu asked me to use proper English, a necessity for these kids if they ever wanted to go to college, which was the ultimate goal even if only a fraction made it there. Not knowing where to start, I noticed a beach ball with a map of the world on it, doubling as a globe. I bounced it between my hands a few times, threw it in the air and caught it, then spun it to the western hemisphere and pointed to home.

"This is where I'm from: Canada." I scanned the room. Fifteen sets of white teeth beamed at me. "Can you say Canada? Ca-na-da?"

"Ca-na-da," they returned in unison with delight.

"My name," I said, pressing my hand on my chest, "is Spencer."

"Spen-sa."

We did this for quite some time—"My name is Spencer. I'm from Canada."—until I was confident they understood.

"Okay," I said. "Who am I?"

"Canada!"

I rubbed my eyes, squinting through the cracks in my fingers at

the months painted on the wall. What value could I possibly provide teaching in a language that only a handful fully comprehended?

I continued with the curriculum I had, teaching about Sierra Leone's utopian origins as the first colony established by slaves freed from Britain (hence the name of the capital, Freetown). I was learning myself as we went, and things were far from smooth. In the middle of one lesson, I heard a boy yelling in pain. He wore a generic yellow soccer jersey and as I approached I saw his fingers were bleeding.

"What are you doing?" I said, urgently grabbing his wrist to see what he held. There was a razor blade in his open, scratched palm. I was alarmed. Why would a child be carrying a razor blade? I looked around the room, baffled, and one-by-one, the other kids started raising their hands—each one holding a razor blade.

I looked back down at the boy in the jersey. He was now also holding a pencil with a rugged tip. He picked up the razor blade and showed me how he shaved the pencil into a point so that he could continue writing.

One of the times that I'd felt entirely absent of control, when I'd been paralyzed and unsure how to make a situation better, came as I stared at a little glob of blood in the toilet, floating in the middle of a milky red web.

Christie sat on the edge of the tub beside it, bent forward, clenching her stomach. She was as pale as the porcelain bath, clammy and feverish, but she wasn't crying. She was, like me, quietly processing.

It was April 2014. We had shared our exciting news for the first time just hours before. We had been visiting with Christie's sister and her family and had told them that Christie was pregnant. Her niece was so excited to have a cousin that her eyes looked like they'd pop from her head. The next day, we were going to drive to see her parents so that we could tell them in person before Christie left for Uganda the next week.

After we got home, though, Christie's voice floated up from the darkness as I lay half-asleep in bed, her words too faint for a message of such gravity: "I'm losing the baby."

I tried to console her, telling her that everything would be okay, that this didn't mean we'd lost the baby. But there was no doubt in Christie's mind—she knew.

As the sun rose, I made tea and brought it to Christie in bed. Mac was there with her, letting Christie comb her fingers through his fur and scratch his ailing body. Nature was taking so much from us.

Over the next few days, I relied on Christie's strength to find my own. We were grateful that her miscarriage had happened at home in Canada, where we had support and facilities at our fingertips, as opposed to when Christie was on her chiropractic mission. Still, there was little to celebrate on the morning of my forty-seventh birthday in April. Our home felt frozen and silent but for Mac, yowling like a broken siren from whichever room he'd huddled in to be alone. Even Chloe sensed the inevitable. She constantly came up and sniffed Mac, checking in on him in a way she'd never done before.

We did our best to administer Mac's IV at home, where he was most comfortable, but he couldn't stand it anymore and he often struggled. As a result, he wasn't getting enough fluids, so we decided to take him to the vet for a full day of treatment.

It was our last day together before Christie left for Uganda. Christie, resilient as ever, had physically recovered and, despite her midwife and doctor's advice, she didn't cancel her plane ticket.

"Are you sure about this?" I asked.

"I made a commitment," she said. "The other doctors are relying on me to go." She was a bit weak and tired still, but she felt it would be a good distraction from the sadness at home. Christie loved what she did, and sharing that with children who had little to nothing in jail was a chance to heal the pain she felt. I was in constant awe of her selflessness and resilience.

We were trying to make the most of our last day together before she left for her trip, but we couldn't force happiness.

After school, I picked up Christie and we headed to the clinic to pick up Mac. He seemed to have perked up, greeting us with his shaking tail and that big malamute grin. Before we left, the vet asked that we get his blood urea nitrogen (BUN) levels tested as a precaution to check how well his kidneys were working. She left us alone with Mac in a patient room, where Christie and I sat, stroking his back and each other's arms. Ten minutes later, the vet returned with a manila folder under her armpit.

"Mac's levels are extremely high," she said. "A normal BUN level ranges between 2.5 to 8.9. Mac's is 64.3. His creatinine levels are even more shocking. A normal range is 27 to 124. His levels are . . ." she trailed off. "Over 1,600. I honestly haven't seen anything like it before."

"What does that mean?" I asked, my voice traveling to its upper register. Mac licked my hands, his head nodding as it did when he wanted to nuzzle.

"I know it doesn't look like it right now because he's had a full day of fluids. But make no mistake, Mac is in a lot of pain. He's suffering."

Christie and I looked at each other, the unspoken sitting between us. Would you rather go in excruciating pain or kiss life goodbye in good spirits? I knew what I'd choose, but Mac couldn't speak for himself, leaving us with a heart-rending decision. Did we let him go, an unexpected but peaceful end, or prolong his life—and pain—just to have more time with him? Which was the more selfish act? There was no way of knowing.

It was like jumping off a cliff—we had to make the call and make it now, before we lost the nerve. It escaped me in one rushed exhalation, "Let's do it now." I took a deep breath and exhaled. "While he's still feeling somewhat well."

"Are you sure?" Christie asked.

"I want you to have the chance to say goodbye to him," I said to her.

She silently nodded, her eyes glassy from withholding tears. "I don't want you to go through this alone."

"I just want to know, do you think we're doing this for ourselves or for Mac?" I asked. I wanted her medical and ethical expertise.

"Spencer," she said, "it's not fair to Mac to let him suffer, even another minute, just to give us more time with him. He's feeling good right now, so . . ." she said, her voice fading.

We signed some paperwork and stayed in the examination room. Mac plopped himself on a towel in the center of the room and lay his head flat, at this point knowing the drill for intravenous drugs. But of course, this dosage would be different.

The doctor inserted a sedative IV into Mac's front leg and left us alone while it took effect. Mac immediately became relaxed and drowsy. His shaking tail slowed gradually. I cupped his chin and, between each kiss on his forehead, repeated, "I love you so much buddy," in a cracked voice. I tried to imprint the feeling of Mac's body on mine. He'd been a happy part of every one of my days for thirteen years—I loved him unconditionally.

"You are the gentlest, sweetest little guy," Christie whispered to Mac. She moved her hands from Mac to me, sensing that I was the one who needed consoling. Unlike me, she'd grown up with dogs and cats whom she'd lost over the years. They all hurt, but nothing hurts as bad as the first loss. This was unbearable for me.

The door clicked open and the vet returned with pursed lips. She filled a syringe with a clear dosage of pentobarbital and inserted it into Mac's IV.

My face was buried in Mac's fur as my wails reached a pitch that even I could tell was unearthly. I only lifted my head when I felt Christie's hand on my shoulder once more. When I opened my eyes, I saw that Mac's were closed. It looked as though he had simply drifted to sleep. When the vet told us he was gone, I didn't believe it. Or I couldn't believe it.

Christie had never seen me cry, and I had thought she never would.

But there was nothing I could do to alleviate the intense pressure in my chest. Suddenly, I was sobbing, my mouth cast wide by grief. Snot bubbled from my nose, adding to my embarrassment. What is it that I was so ashamed of? Crying when I was raised to be stoic, or grieving a pet so viscerally?

It seemed like the right thing to do, but as we left, I would have given anything to make that decision again. To have just one more day with Mac.

Chloe lay next to me on the sectional, panting, back from wandering the house for the tenth time, looking for Mac, her brethren.

After we returned home from putting down Mac, Chloe immediately charged me and buried her nose in my legs, as she always did. But instead of trying to make an escape to the patch of oats for a little snack, she just circled the truck. She probably wondered, *Why aren't I tussling with my companion? And why isn't he here now, trying to filch something from my shrine of bones in the backyard I so love to protect?* With Mac absent, she just wasn't herself, and neither was I.

It felt like a tremendous amount of happiness had evaporated from my life. I tried to channel relief and remind myself that Mac was out of his suffering. But it was a slow healing process.

A few days later, after Christie had left for Uganda, the sun beamed brightly, melting the snow into torrents that streamed across the trails, reminding me of the Rocky Mountains. I decided to take Chloe for a walk to see if it would clear my mind. It was nice to be outside in a T-shirt again, as the snow crunched under our feet. I tried to keep myself from looking behind us, expecting to see Mac go storming past with his funny gait, kicking his back leg off to the side.

Up ahead of me, something piqued Chloe's curiosity. I caught up and crouched to see what she was sniffing. It was a tuft of hair from where I'd brushed Mac's coat last week on the trail.

My face took on so many strange shapes, trying to hold it back,

but the dam broke again and I wept. I fell onto my knees, clutching his fur, my sobbing echoing through the woods like a distant animal. When it was over, when my grief and guilt gauge hit empty, I was overcome with the feeling that we weren't alone. Not in an ethereal sense, but a visceral one—someone was watching us.

I craned my neck to the sky and saw a pair of big, round, yellow eyes. A great horned owl was perched on a birch branch that was beginning to bud, a branch so low I could probably stand and touch the bird's ashy feathers. It was unfazed by my outburst. It stared at me silently, as if daring me to get on my feet again.

So I did. I placed my hands on my wet jeans and pushed myself up. As I rose, the owl, as silent as the coming night, spread its surprisingly wide wings and disappeared into the forest. As it vanished, I felt my pain for Mac subside. I remembered that life is a dash—the dash between two dates: the date you are born and the date you leave. I pulled myself together. Mac's time had ended, but there were so many others I was fortunate to have in my life—Christie, Chloe, Manno—and I knew I had to savor every moment I had with each and every one of them.

Chapter seven

"Our prime purpose in this life is to help others. And if you can't help them, at least don't hurt them."

—14TH DALAI LAMA

While Christie was away in Uganda, I threw myself back into Manno's rescue efforts. I was still firing off inquiries to any contact I could find, but I had little to show for it. Then, one day, I opened my email and found an unusual message. It was from Jason Mier, the executive director of Animals Lebanon, a group against animal rights abuses in the Middle East.

Dear Spencer,

Your email came as a bit of surprise as I just went to Iraq some weeks ago because of this chimpanzee. I had a meeting with the KRG Minister of Agriculture and am still following up . . .

In his email, Jason explained that he had been on the case of Manno and his mysterious "brother" in Erbil since October 2013, ever since a couple of zoo visitors had notified him of two suspiciously young chimpanzees captive in Kurdistan. One Kurdish woman had sent him pictures of both chimps, which Jason attached to the email. There was Manno—even younger than he was when we

met—and the other chimp, who was in terrible shape. Left in a tiny, concrete enclosure without shade from the scorching sun, he looked to be developing white rashes and losing his hair. The woman had complained to the Erbil mayor and then, when she returned to the zoo with a teddy bear and skin nourishment for the chimp, the ape was gone.

Whether Manno's "brother" was in a better place or not was unknown. The zoo staff later claimed the chimp had been sent back to Syria, which seemed dubious at best. But it was enough for Jason to get started. His first inquiry with the prime minister's office was quickly deflected to the tourism ministry, who said they weren't authorized to help because zoos were private enterprises. Jason then tried the agriculture department, which acknowledged the existence of the two "monkeys" that came by smuggling.

By March 2014, we had a plan in place. Jason flew to Erbil to meet with the agriculture minister and, we hoped, Ramadan. The minister was receptive and open to changing zoo standards with Jason's help. He admitted to knowing little about zoos in Kurdistan, but agreed that owners should improve conditions or else shut their doors. He even invited Jason to continue working with the Kurdish Regional Government to educate them on best practices for animal care.

The ministry claimed that Ramadan had never received permission to import an ape. In that case, Manno was "officially" under the control of the ministry, and they hoped Ramadan would release Manno on goodwill alone. If not, they would confiscate him.

"I asked when the confiscation could take place and if it is possible on this visit," Jason told me over the phone using WhatsApp late one evening. "The minister said, 'Do not wait until tomorrow—do it today or the chimpanzee might disappear.'" Jason thanked the minister and agreed to return the next day with Manno.

And then things started falling apart.

The first suspicious sign was when a government driver snubbed Jason, forcing him to head straight to Duhok from Erbil alone in a

cab. On the drive, Jason called the other contacts given to him by the minister—two civil servant veterinarians tasked with helping him coordinate Manno's release—but they wouldn't answer. Likewise, his contacts at the Duhok governor's office had little time for him.

"They kept urging us not to involve the governor and to just speak to the zoo owner instead," Jason said. "Then they said we should try on Monday, as it was getting late in the day—it was only one p.m.!" He called the secretary to the agriculture minister, but she couldn't reach him. Other staff told him the same thing. "I had the feeling that what the minister said was not going to be followed through on."

Jason decided to stick with the plan regardless, showing up at the Ministry of Agriculture office in Duhok, as instructed, to meet the head veterinarian in Duhok Province. "It was the same thing: they were nice enough but no one was willing to confiscate Manno." The vet denied any knowledge of the minister's decision to confiscate Manno. They wouldn't even take Jason to the zoo. In fact, the vet tried dissuading Jason from going to see Manno and Ramadan at all, or from taking any pictures of the zoo if he did.

"Is it a cover-up?" I asked.

"I don't think so," Jason replied. "Everybody there was just getting on with their lives," he explained. "I come out of nowhere and say, 'There's this problem, I need help, and it's going to affect someone in your area very directly.' There's little incentive for local government to act." Jason told me that his group saw the same thing happen all the time with law enforcement in smaller communities, especially with police officers who had to enforce laws in the same communities they lived in, often against the very people they knew and grew up with. "A minister might issue some piece of paper, but the local guy gets blamed and, if something goes wrong, it falls on him."

I understood how that could happen in a village setting, but Duhok was a quarter of a million people—the third-largest city in Iraqi Kurdistan. Then again, the number of people there dealing directly with the agriculture ministry was small, meaning they probably

knew each other closely; definitely better than they would some North American parachuting in, like Jason or me.

It was clear that the vet wasn't going to take Manno into their control. "At this point," Jason said, "it's probably better to continue to the zoo and meet the owner to explain our position ourselves."

I shuffled to the edge of my office chair, hoping that reaching out to Ramadan and the zoo directly would bring about a happy ending or give us a long-awaited update on my friend Manno. But Jason deflated my excitement.

"I fear the worst, Spencer," he said. "If the bureaucrats inform the zoo owner that we're coming, Manno can disappear, and the case will suddenly be forgotten by everyone until everything quiets down, and then Manno will go on display again. I've heard of it happening before in other zoos."

Those fears were top of mind when Jason drove to the Duhok Zoo the next day, along with two bureaucrats sent by the agriculture minister to assist him with negotiations and translations. When Jason arrived, Ramadan was waiting for him at the entrance. He cordially welcomed them into his office, poured them Turkish coffee, and brought Manno out to see them.

Because Manno made so much noise in his cage at night, Ramadan had started paying the caretaker—a Syrian refugee living in an apartment on the premises—to look after him at night. Manno soon became like part of the caretaker's family. It sounded heartening, but I knew that the longer Manno stayed there, the greater the likelihood of something going wrong. If Manno were to inadvertently hurt one of the caretaker's kids or become distressed and attack someone, the blame would fall on him—not the humans who thought it was a good idea to take him out of the wild and place him in an apartment.

After Jason saw Manno, Ramadan opened a folder that was already waiting on his desk. He showed them a document from June 2013, written on official Directorate of Duhok Veterinary letterhead

and featuring multiple stamps and signatures from the state vet who'd just told Jason not to go to the zoo. One of the bureaucrats translated the Kurdish Badini dialect into English: "According to the request for Mr. Ramadan, the owner of the zoo, he would like to bring (2) chimpanzees, (1) zebra, (3) Siberian tigers, (4) antelopes from Zakho border, according to the law (84) in the year 1936."

It seemed that Ramadan had brought Manno to the zoo with all the necessary permissions, all aboveboard.

Jason caught me up on the visit during another one of our online chats. I exhaled with relief hearing that Manno appeared to be healthy and happy. "Did Ramadan say where he got all the animals from?" I asked Jason. I wondered if he had given a different story to Jason than he had to me.

"He said the chimps were brought from Africa to a farm in Syria, but that the area in Syria was now destroyed from the war," Jason said. *That lines up with what he said to me*, I thought.

"Congo. He specifically told me from the Congo," I said.

"A lot of people in the Middle East say the Congo in place of 'jungly Africa,'" Jason explained. "Ramadan wouldn't have that information directly—he'd only have hearsay from whoever was selling to him. If I were to guess, I'd say it was the Ivory Coast, maybe Senegal, because there's a well-documented trade route between there and Syria."

"Even during the civil war?" I asked.

"If anything, the chaos enables it," Jason said. "Normal structures break down. Who is going to spend resources to protect an animal when you have far greater problems? Which isn't to say there's outright bribery, but it does make it easier. I'm moving my cargo through, I know I'm going to make a fortune, giving little tips along the way. Here's a guy at customs who's barely getting paid by the government, so I give him a few dollars. You see?"

I did. "So what happened after Ramadan showed you his documents?"

Despite having legal permission to own Manno, Ramadan said he was willing to part with him. Right then and there. For $20,000.

Jason knew better than to take the deal. Buying a smuggled animal exacerbates the very problem he was trying to solve. If Jason paid Ramadan to rescue Manno, even though Ramadan hadn't broken any Iraqi laws by buying him, it would indirectly reward the smugglers' trade in endangered species. It would also provide Ramadan the funds to buy another chimp—or perhaps two. Instead, Jason offered to leverage his NGO supporters to help Ramadan enrich his zoo: improving the enclosures, training staff, advancing equipment. Anything that would ultimately make the zoo more hospitable for the animals and more educational for visitors, and all of it for free. Ramadan declined and lowered his offer to $15,000, but Jason wouldn't budge—he wouldn't pay for Manno's release. He would not support the illegal animal trade and possibly endanger more animals to save a single primate.

"Ramadan told me, 'Without a court order, I can't give up this animal. But you're welcome to my zoo anytime,'" Jason said. He shook Ramadan's hand and that was the end of it. "If we can't come to an agreement, I have nothing to do but leave. I'm not really a threat, you can't push your way through. You work together, or not at all."

Only, it wasn't the end. It couldn't be.

Years before, Jason had set out to rescue a chimp from Lebanon. It had taken eight years, but he'd got that chimp to safety. Eight years, but he got the job done. I was willing to dedicate even longer to saving Manno—it didn't matter how long it took, Manno deserved a better life, and I would do anything to make that happen. Even better, I knew just who to ask for help.

There's always more that you can do, more you can give. For animals. For people. For this world.

That's the lesson I really grasped in Sierra Leone.

Not long after the incident with the boy sharpening his pencil

with a razor blade, I sat with Mariatu in her family's home and tried to make sense of what I was doing in Sierra Leone.

"I feel useless," I said. "Like I'm just a novelty to the kids. What can I do?"

Mariatu sat quietly for a moment. "You saw those boys using the ditch in the yard as a bathroom?" she asked.

"Yes."

"The teaching will help while you're here, but if you could bring running water to the school, it would greatly improve the lives of these children."

"How much would that cost?"

She hesitated, like it was a number so vast she wasn't comfortable even saying it out loud. After a long pause, she finally said, "Six hundred thousand leones."

I didn't have a way of converting the currency rate. I asked, "How much is that in American dollars?"

"Too, too much," she said. "One hundred and fifty dollars."

It took me a second to register what she said. One hundred and fifty dollars was little more than half a day's work for me as a teacher. "That's it?" I shook my head. "Mariatu, if you want running water, done—let's go get you running water!"

As it turned out, installing running water would be far easier than physically getting the money to pay for it. Nothing is easy in Sierra Leone—not even making a money withdrawal that, back home, could be made from any bank at any hour of any day.

The Kamaras didn't own a vehicle, so getting from their neighborhood, Thunder Hill, to the heart of Freetown required multiple motorcycle taxis and buses—and by buses, I mean large vans packed with two dozen passengers, vehicles where a sliding door would fall off because someone pulled it with too much force or because the driver hit the brakes too hard as he was pulling over. One time, two men walking along the side of the road simply hoisted the door off the street before any passengers could get to it. They put it back on the

rails, clicked it into place, slid it shut, and then went on their way—as if they were just two people politely holding a door for strangers, not installing it.

In total—traffic and door delays and all—it took ninety minutes to get into Freetown. Along the way, Woodie convinced me that no such "automatic transaction machine" of the sort I was describing existed, at least not that he knew of. I'd have to ask Christie to send a money transfer.

Phoning Christie was out of the question. Calls across the vast pond were not easy and were so costly that I wouldn't dare ask Francis to use his cell phone. Instead, Woodie took me to an internet cafe so I could email her.

The crowded shop looked like someone had opened up an internet cafe, cigar room, and sauna in one place. I choked on the smoke fumes and the stench of sweat, trying to find a free computer and, as luck would have it, found one near a small electric fan blowing from the corner of the ashy concrete floor. After spending thirty minutes merely trying to log online, I understood why this computer was so lonely. All I needed to do was email my wife, but the machine processed my commands as slowly as if I were trying to calculate the volume of dark matter in the universe.

I spent about an hour emailing Christie, telling her all about my adventure, and just as I was about to get to my request for money, the power blew. All the screens flashed black and the fans slowed to a stop. We waited for the power to return, but the intense humidity drove us outside.

We eventually found another cafe, where I rapidly pumped out a briefer version of the same email and hit send, praying it worked. We arrived back in Thunder Hill hours later, the task of sending an email having taken the entire afternoon and part of the evening.

The next day, Woodie accompanied me to the same internet cafe, where I was relieved to see Christie had responded with a money transfer control number to receive the money from Western Union.

The only problem was that there was no record of the transaction at the center—the Western Union's lone computer was down. The next day was no better.

My charitable gesture was starting to feel like a burden on Woodie, who chaperoned me wherever I traveled. So, despite the family's warnings the next day, I set off on my own to Freetown, following the same taxi and bus routes. I arrived without incident, and thankfully, the Western Union's computer was running. I hid the cash in a secret pocket I'd sewn on the inside of my pants, but the bulge made by a roll of bills worth 1.2 million leones wasn't very subtle.

I squeezed into a rickety bus with "The Lord Is My Shepherd" painted on its nose in red block letters, and a little while later, I was back with the Kamaras. I had such a rush giving the money to Mariatu, knowing that this would make things a little bit better for the students at the school. For a single act to add real, life-changing value to people's lives—that was a high I hadn't felt before.

The truth is—and I had tried to confess as much to Mariatu—that the teachers who sent themselves across the world for volunteer missions such as mine weren't always that effective. How could we be when we didn't speak the language and knew little to nothing of the curriculum. I was more of a passing distraction for the students, but I wanted to be more. I wanted to distribute as much good as possible, so Mariatu and I made a list of needs for the school—from pencil sharpeners to an internet connection—that I could help procure from back home.

The family had personal needs, too. Gabriel had a bulge in his cheek because of an untreated cavity that had swollen to the size of a golf ball. The total cost for dental care? Five dollars. Granted, as I later learned, "dental care" meant getting the tooth yanked with pliers and no freezing, so I wasn't surprised that Gabriel held on to the $5 for the rest of the time I was there.

It was incredible how far money stretched there. The family's live-in helper, Ruth, wanted to get a certificate in marketing. Done—Christie

and I bought her college tuition at a cost that would make every debt-laden student in the developed world green with envy.

It became incredibly apparent to me that what is, by Western standards, very little could have such a life-changing effect on others. That lesson was hammered home when one of the family's neighbors, a sweet girl named Sarah, told me she had dreams.

"What kind of dreams?" I asked, expecting her to say she wished to become a doctor or an astronaut.

"All I've ever wanted was to have my own notebook," she said.

I couldn't believe it. It seemed such a simple request, but Sarah was being sincere. "I promise, when I get home, I'll send you the most beautiful notebook I can," I said. I made a mental note to ask Christie's scrapbooking friend to help me personalize something to mail to Sarah.

With a few days left before the end of my trip, there was one last thing I wanted to give back to Rhema. I wanted to connect them with the world through the internet. The school had a computer, but it was so old and buggy, it was barely used or useful. After asking around Freetown, I found one person confident he could get the internet to Thunder Hill. He arrived on my last day in the country, along with a new computer for the school, and after eight hours of troubleshooting, Rhema Preparatory School was in touch with the world.

After my last dinner in Sierra Leone, Francis and I retreated to the front porch, where we sat under the cloudy night sky. We did this every night. Francis and I would talk late into the night while we admired the stars together, or commented on a spider spinning a web in the corner of the veranda, or listened to the rain. The conversations flowed until we were too tired to share another laugh, story, or thought. But that night was extra special. The love between me and my host family—adopted children and all—made me wistful for Christie. I hadn't heard her voice, let alone seen her, for weeks, and my heart-to-hearts with the Kamaras made me realize how we sometimes took each other for granted.

Noticing the absence of my smile, Francis asked me what was wrong.

"I miss my wife," I said. "It's hard to go so long without hearing from her."

He nodded his head and put a reassuring hand on my leg. "Yes, it is very hard to be away from the family. You don't know what is happening in their lives."

"That's right," I said.

"Are they happy, are they safe?"

"Yes."

"I understand you. When I was in Nigeria, studying to become a pastor, I saw on the television that the RUF entered Thunder Hill. I heard that they captured one bishop, and we shared a boundary with his house. I panicked, broken in the heart. I wanted to come back, but they closed the airport—there was no flight to Freetown, and I didn't even have money. There was no number I could call to hear from Mariatu and the children. I knew not of what was happening with them. My only option was to lift my eyes to the Lord in an unceasing prayer—day and night—for God's protection on my family.

"After two weeks, Mariatu contacted me. She told me they escaped and were camping in a school room, but they were safe. They stayed there for a month, and I was finally able to return and see them three months later. The Lord was so faithful I did not lose any of my family."

I stared at Francis in disbelief, not only because of the harrowing memory, but because he thought it was even remotely relatable to what I was feeling. My sadness for missing Christie turned to guilt and relief, knowing I lived in a part of the world where I could be away from her for a month and never worry about her safety.

Lightning filled the sky and it started to rain, first like a leaky tap, then a trickle, then a shower as if the heavens had broken open. Francis just put his arm around me and sang through a smile.

The next day I was in a Starbucks lineup at Chicago's O'Hare

Airport. In front of me, a large, suited man reprimanded a poor barista because she didn't get his order right, and I felt utterly culture shocked. When you've just returned from a place that's suffered one of the most horrendous genocides in recent memory, yet where people still laugh and smile and sing unprompted, it makes you wonder why we find it so hard to come by gratitude.

Christie arrived back from Africa just after midnight. She was wide awake—her body still on Ugandan time and imagining it was a bright sunny morning near the equator. Even after enduring a day of flights and jet lag, she still managed to smile an enormous grin as her feet touched the bottom of the escalator and we locked eyes.

We shared a warm embrace and kiss. She looked around the arrivals terminal, blinking as she took in the bright lights, clean floors, orderly crowds, and relative affluence hanging off the shoulders of almost everyone around her. I knew well the unique look of culture shock on her face.

We walked to the car, and I let her decompress on the forty-five-minute drive home. At home, Christie curled up under a blanket on the couch. I brought her a cup of tea and slipped my legs under the blanket across her lap. Chloe found us and climbed on the couch, curling herself into the nook of my back.

"How was it?" I asked.

"Intense," she said. "I spent every day in a children's prison or part of town that looked more like a garbage dump than a neighborhood to me."

"And the kids?" I asked.

"They loved it. I don't know if it was the adjustment itself or just having someone put their hands on them with good intentions, but they absolutely loved it." She laughed. "Some of them tried fooling us by getting back in line for another turn. Cheeky little guys."

"And you—how was it for you?"

"Very healing for me," she said. Christie told me about visiting the Kigali Genocide Memorial in neighboring Rwanda, where she paid tribute to 250,000 Tutsi, and how the entire trip made her feel so undeservedly privileged to be Canadian. "But how are you feeling?" she asked me.

"I've been busy," I said. "I've been talking a lot with a guy named Jason in Beirut. Primate expert and genuinely amazing guy."

"Is he going to help you with Manno?"

"No, I'm going to help *him*. He really knows what he's doing."

I told Christie all about Jason. The first time I'd seen Jason on video chat, I'd been somewhat surprised by the man I was meeting. The persistent animal rights fighter, a thorn in so many zookeepers' and politicians' sides, was a soft-spoken man in his thirties with shoulder-length light brown hair and a slim mustache. His humble demeanor defied his assertive nature. As a youngster in Flint, Michigan, Jason grew up around chickens and turkeys and many pets. Like me, he was raised in a farming community, spending time at his grandparents' dairy farms and peeling back the pages of their *National Geographic* magazines on boring summer days. The pictures of wild animals, rescued or hunted, endangered or prosperous, captivated him. When he was as young as ten years old, he knew he wanted to be on the other side of the world, helping animals however he could.

I admired Jason immensely. Before he was in junior high, he'd figured out what had taken me decades to realize—the value of a global education, the rights of animals, the interconnectedness of everyone and everything in this world.

"He left to work for NGOs in West Africa at twenty-two years old," I told Christie. "Then he moved to Spain to care for chimpanzees in a sanctuary, and he never looked back. It was his calling."

"How did he end up in Lebanon?" she asked.

"He moved there because of one specific chimp he was hell-bent on getting out of a terrible situation."

"You better not be planning a move to Iraq."

"If it brings you any comfort, the chimp was only half the reason he moved there. The other was a Lebanese woman—his wife, Maggie."

Christie gave me a supportive squeeze and tucked her head under my chin. For a while, we snuggled quietly, listening to the steady cadence of the piano ballad "Say Something" by A Great Big World and Christina Aguilera. The simple, but powerful and painful lyrics drifted around us. At that moment, the words seemed to be speaking directly to us.

The song evoked such intense emotion, Christie's eyes welled up with tears. When the final verse finished, she broke down.

Finally, she looked up at me, smiling as she gazed into my eyes. "I'm ready to try again," she said.

Chapter eight

"An animal's eyes have the power to speak a great language."

—MARTIN BUBER, TWENTIETH-CENTURY
PHILOSOPHER

The fall of 2014 was passing with a calmness that had been absent earlier that spring. Christie was just past the twelve-week mark of her pregnancy, which so far had come with few complications. We were thankful for the peace and tried to make the most of it.

One of our favorite activities was to simply take long walks through the forest beside our house, under the auburn-and-honey-colored canopies. We often brought one of the dogs—Chloe or Emma (but never together)—with us. Chloe was getting on in years, but she still defended her position as the top dog in the house and remained contemptuous of any canine roommates, to say the least.

Walking with Emma through the winding country paths around our home, my thoughts inevitably made their way back to Manno. If it hadn't been for Emma, I would never have even considered being able to rescue him. Of the many lessons I was learning, the most important was that you have to leave doors open to different futures. Otherwise, you'll never find the hidden roads of your life.

Just as with Manno, the road that brought me to Emma was

completely coincidental. I met Emma in 2009. That summer, I arrived in Kabul, Afghanistan's capital city, where I would be spending the next month as a volunteer teacher.

My placement was with the Aschiana Foundation, which was founded as an informal school for street children who had been forced to leave school to help support their families. The school's founder, Yousef Mohamed—affectionately known as "Engineer Yousef" on account of the profession he had before dedicating his life to his country's neediest children—believed that the survival of Afghanistan depended on these children's employability and civic engagement.

On my first trip to the campus, I must have seen dozens of the school's students out in the streets, hawking Chiclets and travel-size tissue packs or quickly washing down vehicles for a couple of bills. When I reached the school, the iron gates in the center of a cement wall screeched open and my driver rolled into the compound. Behind me, two guards pulled the gates closed, and the sound of Kabul's traffic melted into the background. Aschiana was an oasis in Kabul's bustling streets, with bright flower gardens and young fruit trees amongst a few converted houses, as well as a big peacock wandering the grounds. It was immediately apparent that this school was better funded than any other I'd volunteered at previously.

I wandered the grounds in search of Yousef. I tried to keep my eyes on the school grounds, but I kept glancing at the sky. My new colleagues didn't bat an eye at an Apache helicopter hovering close overhead, or the white smoke tracing the trajectory of two rockets launched from it. The stringy plumes of white extended in either direction and slowly dissolved into the sky. It was so surreal that for a few seconds I just blinked slowly, head still tilted skyward. *We can normalize even the most extreme of conditions*, I thought.

I didn't find Yousef, but he eventually found me—the only six-foot blond white man staring at the sky.

"*As-salaam alaykum*," he said, placing his hand lightly on his

chest, a long white robe flowing behind him. An unassuming man with a kindhearted smile framed by a thick, neatly trimmed beard, Engineer Yousef had a calmness to him that defied the years of terror and intimidation he'd survived while living in Kabul, first under Taliban rule and now inside a war zone.

Before I even met Yousef, I admired and respected his selflessness and bravery. When Yousef founded the first Aschiana school in 1995, it was open to boys and girls. A short time later, he arrived at work to find Taliban officials inspecting the schoolhouse. It wasn't an unusual situation under the oppressive regime, but that didn't make it any less dreadful. Yousef was promptly arrested by the men and hauled to prison. His head was shaved, and he was thrown into a darkened cell with only a pinpoint of light shining through at the apex of the cement-walled room. He shared the claustrophobic surroundings with twenty other men. Each lived in fear of having his name called, a signal of hastening fate that might include execution, dismemberment, or simply a vague "disappearance." Many days passed before Yousef's name was finally called and he was brought before a Taliban judge. Thankfully, the positive effects of his work had imprinted themselves on the community. Dozens of supporters sat in the courthouse and parents of his myriad students testified in support of his character. His life was spared, but only on the condition that he cease teaching girls. With the overthrow of the Taliban in 2001, Aschiana had immediately resumed teaching girls, but there was still an element of risk in doing so, as remnants of fundamentalism still prevented some parents from enrolling their daughters.

Yousef arranged for a driver to take me to my off-campus home for the next few weeks. While he waited for the driver, he explained, "We picked this house for you because it is unlikely to be hit by rockets."

"Thank you," I said, unsure of what else to say.

When I arrived at the home, a suite in a walled-in, motel-like

compound, I could practically see the heat ripples radiating off the walls. There was a large pool that looked refreshing, so long as you could get over the floating layer of slime. (And by day fifteen of oppressive heat, I could.)

Yousef had asked me not to venture out at night due to the high incidence of kidnappings, the possibility of stray bullets, and collateral damage from VBIEDs (vehicle-borne improvised explosive devices) in the area. That night, as I went to bed, I made a mental note of the best escape route from my room and placed my shoes directly beside my bed in case the need for a hasty exit arose.

A few nights later, as I was returning from Aschiana, I heard a *whack* and a whimper. I turned to see a shopkeeper shooing away a pure white dog with a broom handle. The poor thing was skin, bones, and teats—a mother probably trying to nourish herself for her pups or scrounge together some food for them. The pink of her skin was visible through her ivory fur. As she scampered toward a ditch, I approached her as I would Mac and Chloe, by kneeling down with extended hands.

Her eyes sought mine and she hopped toward me, nuzzling in the crook of my lap and rolling onto her back for belly rubs. The fleas skipping across her protruding ribs weren't a bother to me. I missed my dogs too much to resist this cuddle-monger. This one deserved, as all dogs do, a little affection, a pet, and some kindness.

I vowed to bring her some food scraps if I saw her again, though I knew it wouldn't be *halal*. The next morning, I discreetly balled up a bit of my breakfast in a napkin and smuggled it out of the guesthouse, so as not to attract any attention. When I neared the shop, there was the dog. I knelt down and opened the napkin, and she greedily ate up the bread, meat, and fruit inside. It became a morning ritual, and each time the dog saw me, her body would begin vibrating and her tail thumping against the ground. She'd lap up the rice I'd brought her or trot down a busy road with naan clenched in her jaws.

One evening, I walked back toward that noisy road. As I neared her usual spot, I heard a squeaking from the gutter. I peered down and saw that the mother had given birth to a litter of puppies. In hindsight, it wasn't my brightest moment, given how dark it was and Yousef's many warnings against putting myself in easy-to-kidnap situations. It was hard to feel scared, however, looking down at the wriggling white mass of fur in the ditch. I hopped down and sat on the incline, and the puppies immediately started falling over me, licking my face, and crawling over each other. Fleas had ravaged their skin, which left them with wounds from scratching, and several pups now had maggots inhabiting their cuts.

I returned over the following days with a big cardboard box, but each time, neither mama nor the pups were there. The day had become overcast and muggy, and the gutter was an oozing bog reeking of sewage. I slid down the edge of the ditch, called out for the dogs, and waded in until I spotted them backed up within a culvert. I reached in and fought to grab a tuft or tail, but the puppies kept wriggling out of my grip.

I finally crawled out of the culvert just as it started to pour. Sheets of rain pelted my face as I squinted up at a group of Afghan men gathering above, laughing at the crazy white man crawling through a putrid ditch. With the dogs in the box, I crawled back aboveground. It took some effort, but a cab finally agreed to take me to the veterinary clinic, provided the dogs rode in the trunk.

I presented the two Afghan veterinarians with the pups and explained that I would pay for any flea medication and ointments to heal their scabs and ease their suffering, plus a round of vaccines. When I explained that I'd rescued them from a ditch, I half expected the doctors to roll their eyes, but they were immensely accommodating and refused to accept my pay. This wasn't the Middle Eastern custom of feigning generosity as part of a negotiation; this was a sincere reminder that there was abundant goodwill everywhere.

Yousef agreed to house the dogs at Aschiana for a few days, despite

a no-dogs policy. "Just until they find homes," he clarified as we set up a large plywood crate for them in an old work shed on the school grounds.

Before I made my way back to my guesthouse, I heard a familiar whimpering on the opposite side of the gates. I opened the solid metal gate and saw the mother staring up at me longingly, crying for her pups. I'd traveled from the ditch to the vet and back, and somehow, through might or miracle, she'd tracked her puppies' whereabouts to the school. Yousef made yet another exception to the rules and allowed her into the compound.

"Until they find homes," he reminded me.

"Yes, until they find homes," I repeated.

A day or two turned to a week, and as my departure date loomed, I knew I had to find a place for them. I was quickly running out of time in Kabul, but just before I left, I was able to find all of the dogs—mother and puppies—safe haven with an NGO who agreed to look after the dogs until we could find them homes in Canada.

Looking at Emma on one of our walks in 2014, I was amazed at how far she had come. It had taken the better part of two years, but we'd managed to fly all of the dogs to Canada and find amazing families for the puppies. All of her pups were now fully grown and had loving homes. Emma, of course, had come to live with me, Christie, Mac, and Chloe.

"Remember how many times I thought we'd never get them here?" I asked Christie as we walked the trails with Emma.

"A hundred?" said Christie. "Hundred and one?"

"But we did it," I said. The logistics and cost had been daunting beyond anything I had ever undertaken. I had no idea how we would ever pull it off until we finally did.

I felt confident that there were some overlapping lessons in persistence and awareness-raising that would help me with my latest rescue mission, and I was optimistic that a similarly peaceful future was in store for Manno. Despite Jason Mier being sent away from Duhok

Zoo empty-handed and Ramadan challenging him and the Ministry of Agriculture, there was reason to believe Ramadan could be swayed. The Republic of Iraq had recently become the 180th nation to sign CITES. Though CITES was an imperfect organization, it was still a useful ally in protecting further illegal animal smuggling.

I was also encouraged by Jason's recent update. Apparently, the agriculture minister had indicated that he was looking into new ways to confiscate Manno and expedite his release. *We'll get you home, Manno.*

If only wishing made it so. A few days later, our plans were turned on their head when a new agriculture minister was appointed. Suddenly, Manno's case fell off the government's radar. No matter which staff Jason and I contacted, we couldn't get through anymore. All of our calls and emails were ignored. All of the relationship building and hard work we'd put in over the past months went up in smoke.

Even worse, ISIS started advancing on Northern Iraq. Their most recent position was only kilometers from Manno and the Duhok Zoo, putting the Kurdish Peshmerga in the highest gear imaginable and making all other issues in the region a low priority. Given what was at stake, Jason and I felt it was necessary to back off—even a well-intentioned pursuit could come across as callous when there was a war on their doorstep. Tens of thousands of people were killed in the battle for Mosul alone, and the hundreds of thousands of displaced people were making Iraq an extension of Syria's already massive refugee crisis. ISIS's barbaric militia was already trying to seize Kirkuk, a disputed territory between Iraqi Kurdistan and Iraq proper, and there was no reason to think they'd stop there.

On our next call, I hoped Jason might have some sort of silver lining to all the bad news. But there were more clouds on the horizon.

"Are you following news about the energy market?" he asked.

"Following it? I'm living it," I said. The oil market crashed seemingly out of the blue, rumbling throughout the province and resulting in thousands of layoffs and steep government cutbacks.

"Same thing is happening in Kurdistan," Jason said. "Only worse, because their economy isn't as diversified. Government workers' salaries are being cut by a quarter and people are quite upset."

"As if the people of that region haven't been punished enough," I said. "What's this mean for the mission?"

"If you thought animal rights issues were on the back burner before, now they're completely invisible to lawmakers. My contacts there have said as much—there's no more support for Manno's cause."

"The market booms and busts all the time," I said. "We'll just give it some time to bounce back."

"It's not that simple," Jason said gently. "Even if we can get the same level of support again and collect all the permits needed to get Manno out of Iraq, I just don't know if it's safe to go to Duhok in the foreseeable future."

The heinousness of ISIS wasn't as apparent then, so I was less concerned than Jason about my personal safety. *Couldn't be worse than Kabul,* I thought. But I recounted our conversation to Christie on our walk, and she agreed with Jason.

"I admire what you're doing for Manno, and you know you've got my full support, but I am not raising our kid alone," she said. "Jason lives in Beirut—he's seen some things. I think you ought to trust his judgment."

Our acreage came into view as we took the final turn in the path, and I felt the cool air in the shadow of the woods. As Christie opened the garage door, I pulled her in for a kiss and then crouched to embrace and kiss her belly, which had just started showing the slightest bump.

Our child was due in six months, on March fourth. *March forth.* It couldn't be more symbolic of our lives at that moment. I knew Christie was right, but it was hard to accept—I didn't like the idea of just sitting on my hands, not knowing how or when Manno might make it out of a war zone. Parenthood hadn't dampened my resolve to free Manno. If anything, it made me want to right the wrongs done

to Manno even more. I wanted to lead by example for my own child. I wanted him or her to fully understand the transformative power of caring for those beings unable to defend themselves and of never giving up when you know you're doing the right thing, regardless of what anyone says. I had to find a way.

Chapter nine

"For in the true nature of things, if we rightly consider, every green tree is far more glorious than if it were made of gold and silver."

—MARTIN LUTHER

It was hard to believe, but in the last days of September 2014, five months after putting Mac down, we found ourselves in the same clinic, with the same problem, considering the same options.

Emma had become increasingly lethargic over the past few weeks. It had been gradual, so I hadn't noticed the change until a friend pointed it out at the annual reunion for the dogs.

"Emma's looking a little thin," said Clydine, one of the adopters of Emma's pups. We watched for a moment as Emma and her fully grown daughter Snowy horseplayed by our feet. After I'd brought Emma over from Afghanistan, she had plumped up to a healthy size, but now she'd shed a bit of the fat.

"She sure isn't looking like herself," Charlotte, Snowy's adopter, said.

I didn't think much of Emma's behavior that day—I chalked it up to her being happily worn out from all the excitement. But on the drive home, Christie wondered aloud, "When did her weight loss and fatigue start?" She could have been dehydrated on an especially hot day. Or perhaps there had just been too much going on in our lives to see the obvious. Mac's death and Chloe's deteriorating health, the

miscarriage and new pregnancy, and not to mention my efforts to rescue Manno, had kept my mind more than occupied. Was it possible that we missed critical signs that something was wrong with Emma?

We hoped that her exhaustion was temporary—a symptom of something she ate that wasn't sitting well with her. But after some preliminary tests at Dr. Greenbank's clinic, the diagnosis came in: renal failure. Just like Mac. We took Emma home to see how she responded to her intravenous fluid over the next couple days, which she mostly spent in an open-door crate that she was all too eager to make into her sanctuary.

I was in utter disbelief that this could happen to a six-year-old dog. However lethargic Emma was, every thump of her tail against the floor was enough to fuel my denial and give me hope. Sadly, after three days of virtually nonstop, around-the-clock IV treatment, Emma's kidneys had only gotten worse.

I spent most of those days pampering her. Emma would perk up whenever Christie brought her some warm cooked ground beef, nibbling the meat from Christie's hands. One night, she ate three bowls full until she couldn't possibly swallow another bite.

On her last day on earth, Emma slept on our bed and we stroked and kissed her face. Her trainer, Leanne, who so lovingly looked after Emma when we weren't home, came by to say a tearful goodbye, as well. I wanted to remember everything about Emma, all the idiosyncrasies. Her stubby little ears. The faint discoloration on the top of her cropped tail that could wag in circles like a helicopter when she was excited. Her piercing eyes and the thin black line of a scar that ran vertically over her right eye socket. We rubbed the bristles on her pink, freshly shaven belly that had once nursed those nine puppies in a gutter in Kabul.

It was Emma who'd taught me, all those years ago, that my true passion was helping animals. I treasured my experiences as a teacher and what I was able to do in that role, but after I brought Emma and her puppies over, I had come to realize that my heart belonged to the animals around me. Chloe and Mac had first unlocked the door all those years earlier, and Emma had kicked it down. There were countless people around the world who needed help, of course, and

I wished I could do something for every one of them. But I had also come to realize that there was a fundamental difference when it came to the value we placed on the life of an animal. I felt compelled to be one of the voices for them.

When Emma died, on September 30, 2014, my purpose was thrown into doubt again. Nothing had moved on Manno's case. The Kurdish economy had worsened, and the Iraqi army had lost more ground to ISIS's offensive. Now, the thought of carrying on trying to rescue Manno without Emma's inspiration at my side was a mountain I wasn't sure I could climb. The enormous effort and emotional commitment that Manno's rescue demanded, all while I was about to become a father, were taking a toll.

It wasn't long after losing Emma that Christie, my guiding light, suggested I do something unusual.

"You need some perspective," Christie said. "Maybe you should finally try an ayahuasca retreat like you've talked about."

I wasn't surprised Christie encouraged me. I'd been talking about ayahuasca for months, ever since hearing some UFC fighters talking about how they used it. Though I do think Christie thought I was nuts when I first described it to her.

"Why the sudden change of heart?" I asked.

"You supported me going to Uganda, and I want to support you on your journey," she said. So, we looked at the website of an ayahuasca retreat in Peru.

"It got five stars on AyaAdvisors, the TripAdvisor for ayahuasca retreats," Christie said, with a laugh. "Can't be that crazy of an idea."

That conversation was on a Sunday in October. The following Tuesday, I was on a flight to the Amazon.

On the first night of my retreat—after my body dispelled seemingly every drop of fluid it contained—I made it back to my cabin shortly after midnight. Every muscle in my body felt like it had been stretched and convulsed for hours, though "felt" is an overstatement, considering

how numb the process left me. It was as though I was all consciousness and no body. My brain whirred with the received wisdom I'd come for—that I need not look any further for meaning in life than love—and that, in the end, was beautiful in its simplicity.

I fell asleep reflecting on what I'd learned. All that mattered was that I'd loved Mac and Emma during our time together to the best of my ability. I had confidence that if I continued to love Manno, we would find a way to get him out of captivity. And I knew that my love for Christie was about to lead to a new type of love that I wouldn't truly understand until our child was born.

The following day, I made the long journey down the Amazon River to the nearby city of Iquitos. Christie had sent a message: "Chloe's not well. Experiencing vertigo and falling over. Can't get up."

This wasn't the first time Chloe had lost her ability to stand, but it was worrisome nonetheless. *She could be gone by the time I'm home*, I thought. After losing Mac and Emma, I was convinced that I would never see Chloe again.

That night, during my second ceremony in the hut, huddled with my bucket on a mattress under the night sky, I tried to come to terms with the idea that we might lose Chloe and that I might not be there when it happened. My thoughts kept coming back to her, the good and the bad. Soon, I could see Chloe by my side, looking at me intensely with her golden eyes. *Don't be so hard on people*, her expression seemed to tell me. *Don't be so hard on your child.*

A couple of days later, as I sat on the plane back to Edmonton, I reflected on what I'd seen. There are infinite lessons that can improve our lives, it's just a matter of letting them find us. The ayahuasca brew helps put those lessons on a fasttrack, but it's life itself that's the real ceremony. The ayahuasca ceremony showed me where I needed to put in the work, but I knew it was up to me to follow through.

For the next five months after I returned from the Peruvian jungle, things moved along smoothly. Christie had been feeling relatively fine

and there were no complications with her pregnancy. Chloe seemed healthy, too, and she hadn't had any more episodes. Christie's due date quickly approached, and then passed. At first, we weren't concerned, but eight days later, our child (we didn't know the sex, nor had we come to an agreement on any two names) still hadn't arrived, so Christie booked an appointment with her midwife that afternoon.

Christie spent the morning in bed, counting the baby's kicks. By the third trimester, a woman can typically count ten kicks in two hours. Christie felt none. At the birthing center, her midwife detected only the faintest heartbeat and observed that her belly was smaller than the week before, so she went for an ultrasound.

After running the ultrasound test, the technician said, "I'm just going to confer with a doctor and then you can get dressed and go." Twenty minutes passed and Christie grew increasingly concerned. When the tech finally returned with a doctor, they wasted no time.

"You're going to have this baby today," said the doctor. "You need a C-section."

"No, I'm not," said Christie. Christie had imagined a home delivery in a birthing pool with her midwife, doula, and me, a birth that would be as serene as humanly possible.

The doctor explained that the baby was frank breech—he was jackknifed. As a result, he was "brain sparing," a condition where all his energy went to the brain and nothing to the body. The result was that our baby had a body that measured as though it was thirty-seven weeks old and a head that measured forty-four weeks.

"He has to come out immediately," the doctor said. "We're taking you to a room right now."

Christie contacted her midwife and me. Her midwife arrived immediately. Unfortunately, my phone was on silent, and I didn't receive her calls—all ten of them.

By the time I looked at my phone a couple of hours later, there was a torrent of messages from Christie and her family.

I called Christie, and the agony in her voice as she answered the phone turned my stomach upside down.

"What happened?" I asked, fearing the worst.

"I need to have a C-section," she said between sobs. "There's something wrong with the baby."

Her words sent me into a near panic attack. I rushed to the hospital. I still don't know how I got there accident free, let alone in thirty minutes.

When I burst into the hospital room, Christie lay on a gurney, more composed than she had been on the phone, which helped calm my nerves. Moments later, her doctor entered the room. "Okay, Christie, let's walk to the operating room."

Christie and I laughed, but the doctor didn't. "Are you kidding?" she asked.

"Seriously, you're walking in," said the doctor.

My wife and I exchanged a bemused look. I shrugged and with the doctor's help, got Christie up off the stretcher and on her feet. With her arms around us, we waved to her family gathered in the hallway some distance away and she wobbled into the operating room. Christie lay down and the medical team extended a fabric obscuring my view of her belly.

"You can watch," the doctor told me. "This will all be very quick." She patted me on the shoulder and sent me to the other side of the fabric.

Thankfully, the surgery went smoothly, and at 7:11 p.m., our child was born: a son.

"This probably would not have ended well for either mom or baby had this happened naturally," the doctor said before leaving. I thanked her, once again feeling privileged to live where I did.

When you're expecting your first child, other parents will repeat a cliché to you: once they're born, you won't be able to imagine your life without them. I had always nodded knowingly when I heard it, but it wasn't until I held our son in my arms for the first time and stroked his fine blond hair that I felt the truth of those words. When I left for home that evening, we still hadn't decided on a name. I called Christie.

"What should we name him?" I asked her.

"I know you like Anders," she said.

"It was my great-grandfather's name," I replied. "Do you like it?"

I could hear Christie smile. "He looks like an Anders."

I was surprised by how calm Anders was from the start. Friends with babies described how they'd felt like absolute wrecks from lack of sleep for months on end, but our boy slept peacefully, sparing us the excruciating crying sessions friends had warned us about. Christie was in great health, too, and as an unseasonably warm spring began, we felt energized about our new lives together.

Chloe immediately took to Anders when we brought him home, pushing her way between Christie and me to lick his wrinkly newborn face. Chloe's health had been failing, and I was thankful that she could experience our growing family before she inevitably left it. Chloe had always loved children, and after all, she was the one who started it all by helping me meet Christie.

For the next few months, Anders was the only thing that excited Chloe anymore, it seemed. She spent hours lying in her spot by the front door, but anytime she heard Anders coo or cry, she was immediately on her feet, tail slowly swooshing back and forth happily.

The morning of July 19, 2015, for the second consecutive day, I sat beside Chloe in her favorite spot, pushing a bowl of wet dog food under her nose.

"Come on, girl," I said, "just try it." Her breathing was strained, and her eyes stared dully into the distance. She used to gobble her food in a few bites, but this bowl might as well have been empty and me invisible.

I eventually managed to get Chloe outside for a walk. It was a balmy day, not too hot for a dog in her condition, and we strolled down the road. Slow as she was, Chloe took well to the breeze, and there were signs of her old self in the way she sloshed through the puddles in the ditches and sniffed at the plants on the side of the path.

The neighbor's Rottweiler, TJ, barked from their front porch

as we passed. Chloe's nose wriggled in the dog's direction and she bayed violently at it, despite the fact that the other dog was bigger, younger, and no doubt healthier. Part of me was heartened by the sight of Chloe desperate to be her same bully self—I already missed her bossiness and her malamute disobedience. I put my leg in front of her to block her, but she kept bumping into it and falling on her side, like a cranky old man chasing the neighborhood kids with his cane.

Again and again, she knocked herself down, each time taking longer to rise up. Finally, she just rolled on her side and lay in the grass, staring at me like I'd done something wrong. I carried her eighty-five-pound body home, up a steep hill, her legs kicking the whole way. I pushed the door open with my side and carried her inside.

"I'm calling Dr. Greenbank," I said, placing Chloe down gently.

"Today's the day?" asked Christie.

"Today's the day."

When Dr. Greenbank arrived later that afternoon, I hoped for Chloe to be released from this world as peacefully as Mac and Emma. But old habits die hard.

Before she was administered the sedative, Chloe was stumbling around the house, pacing with no destination and panting like she'd just sprinted around the world.

I cradled her head in my arms as the vet slid an IV needle into her paw. Chloe started wailing and thrashing and kicking so vigorously that she knocked out the IV wire. Christie had to help me hold her as the vet reinserted it.

"Please, please, don't feel this, stop suffering," I whispered to her, choking on my tears. "I love you, Chloe-Bear."

The first sedative took effect after what seemed like an eternity. Chloe wailed and fought us. Dr. Greenbank quickly injected two large clear plungers into her paw. A minute later, Chloe went limp as her final breath left her.

There was a rock lodged in my throat—a rock so big it physically

hurt to swallow. I buried my face into Chloe's musty fur, soaking her coat with tears. She was not ready to go. I wasn't ready to let her go.

The world in late 2015 felt tense amid all that was happening in Canada and abroad—the worst refugee crisis since the Second World War, a brittle European Union, a rash of senseless terrorism, proxy wars across the Middle East, and a populist American presidential candidate who announced his run for office with the proclamation that Mexicans were drug dealers and rapists. I was just a young man at the end of the Cold War, but I remembered my shock watching the nightly news then. I caught the same look in my reflection on my smartphone screen when I read the news that fall.

Still, I'd always been an optimist, maybe never more so then since Anders came into our lives. I hadn't given up on getting Manno out of Iraq, and neither had Jason or Cheryl Bernard, who was still working with and advising us. Through Cheryl's connections with the Kurdish prime minister's office and Jason's continued political pressure, we were closer to getting approval to free Manno.

We still had one major problem, though: Where would we take Manno when we had him in our custody?

Manno couldn't simply be returned to the wild. There was no catch-and-release system for great apes snatched from their families, and he had spent too long out of the wild to be able to simply be dropped back into it; he'd never survive without help. Manno was still spending his nights with the zoo caretaker's family, and although that was a step up from his cage atop the snakes, it was by no means a long-term solution.

The only option seemed to be a chimpanzee sanctuary, of which only a handful existed. Most were spread across Africa, Spain, and Brazil, but there was also one in the United Kingdom. The sanctuaries were the closest thing to the Congolese rainforests from whence Manno had come, albeit highly controlled by human caretakers and

primatologists to ensure the health, safety, and proper integration of rescued chimps. The human management was kept to a minimum, but it was a necessity to ensure the chimps formed artificial families, without which the chimps would engage in sometimes fatal fighting.

Securing a spot in a chimp sanctuary was quite the endeavor, though. For one, the cost of caring for one chimp was approximately $20,000 a year, so that ruled out several cash-strapped facilities simply unable to take on the responsibility of caring for another animal. But the bigger obstacle was that, according to CITES's well-intended regulations, trafficked chimpanzees were supposed to return to their country of origin. For Manno, that was likely the Democratic Republic of the Congo, but it was impossible to know for sure. The options for sanctuaries in the DRC were limited, and if none of the organizations there agreed to accept Manno, then we'd have to work extra hard to justify moving him to a nonnative habitat.

I felt stuck. But then I saw an ad on my Facebook feed that caught my eye. It said: "An Evening with Jane Goodall." Jane Goodall—the world's leading primatologist and the founder of the premier institute for the protection of apes—was coming to my city, Edmonton, to give a lecture.

I brought the laptop over to Christie in the living room, patting our sleeping Anders's back as she cradled him. "Have you seen this?" I asked.

Christie gave me a big, knowing smile. "I already got us tickets for the meet and greet," she said. "You can ask for her help."

This is Manno. I looked after him in Iraq and he has been illegally smuggled. We need a place for him to go.

I was rehearsing my lines in my head as I slowly approached Jane Goodall in the book-signing lineup that wound through the large auditorium lobby.

This is Manno. I looked after him in Iraq and he has been illegally smuggled . . .

It was my second attempt at trying to convey this message to her. At the meet and greet before the lecture, I was ready to show her a picture of Manno on my phone and make my plea. But there were so many other "VIPs" who were bombarding her with questions and requests for selfies, tiring her out. I edged closer and closer, getting within a few feet of her, but her handler, perhaps sensing the primatologist's exhaustion, swooped in and ended things prematurely. I understood—Jane had flown in straight from the United Kingdom, no sleep, and remained as polite and gracious as anyone could be. But as I watched her disappear into a back room, I kicked myself for not elbowing my way through the crowd and making my plea.

This is Manno. I looked after him in Iraq . . .

This was my last chance. I prayed I wouldn't fumble my words. I'd rehearsed these twenty-three words for hours. There must have been a thousand people in the line, so I knew I had to be fast.

"This is Manno," I finally said when I reached the front of the line, holding my phone in front of me and speaking rapidly. "Manno is—I mean, I looked after him in Iraq."

"I'm sorry," she said, shaking her head at me wearily. "Who?"

I took a deep breath and tried again, enunciating my spiel carefully and holding the phone upside down so the screen rotated toward her. Jane's gaze locked on Manno's big brown globes in the picture, and her eyes lit up.

"Yes," she said, "I know about this chimp."

"You know this chimp?"

"There's a team trying to get him out at the moment."

"That's us!" I said. "But we haven't had any luck. Please, can you help?"

"Give your information to that woman over there," she said with her famous soft-spoken tone, pointing to the CEO of the Jane Goodall Institute's Canadian branch. "She'll take care of you." She thanked

me, then smiled at the fan behind me eagerly clutching her book. I stepped aside, bewildered and skeptical, unsure whether she was brushing me off or whether change is really that simple when you have the power of Dr. Jane Goodall behind your cause.

Within a month, my friend finally had a place to go: Sweetwaters Chimpanzee Sanctuary. Sweetwaters was one of the world's premier chimpanzee sanctuaries, a 250-acre habitat that had emerged out of a partnership amongst Jane's organization, Kenya Wildlife Services, and Ol Pejeta Conservancy. Since 1993, Sweetwaters had given a second life to thirty-four chimpanzees—every one of them survivors of smuggling, hunting, and the entertainment industry. If everything went well, Manno would be their thirty-fifth.

Once we had Sweetwaters behind us, things started clicking into place more quickly than I ever could have hoped. While Sulaiman put pressure on the Kurdish bureaucrats, Cheryl Bernard continued her personal requests to her friend, none other than Prime Minister Nechirvan Barzani, for help. Instead of confiscating Manno from Ramadan, the prime minister's office negotiated terms for the release of Manno to our care. Ramadan finally agreed. It was incredible that in the middle of a humanitarian crisis, an ISIS advance, and an economic catastrophe, the prime minister had taken the time to hear Cheryl's petition and help what she called his "animal citizen." Barzani's response was telling: "As Kurds, we know what it means to be persecuted."

Having a mutual agreement between Manno's owner and the respected leader of Kurdistan would make the transfer less complicated, but there was still a bureaucratic gauntlet of Kenyan wildlife officials and Kurdish and Iraqi governors to navigate.

Jason, as coordinator of the transfer, mediated between the two governments—a test of both his abilities and tenacity. He had transferred trafficked chimpanzees and other animals many times before. He knew all the red tape and minutiae, from crate sizes and design to airline policies. All I could do now was leave it in the hands of the experts and remain ready to offer whatever help I could.

As a kid, I had dreams of making it in the big leagues—if not the NFL or NHL, then the CFL.

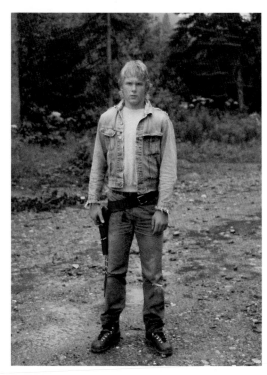

When I wasn't playing sports growing up, my family and I spent a lot of time outdoors, and I learned to fish and hunt. It wasn't until I was older that I stopped hunting.

Christie with Mac, Chloe, and Keena.
Chalice Stewart Photography

Christie and I hiked to the summit of Mount Kilimanjaro in 2011 as a fund-raising effort to bring the Super Seven (dogs we rescued in Afghanistan) back to Canada. *Jerome Kileo*

The Kamara family—(*left to right*) Gabriel Turay, Samuel Kamara, Betty Bundor, Esther Kamara—was my host in Sierra Leone, the first country where I volunteered. Warm-hearted and full of compassion, the family showed me how I could give back to the people around me.

Teaching at Rhema Preparatory School for a summer was one of the most rewarding experiences of my life.

Manno's sleeping crate in the Duhok Zoo was on top of a crate of snakes. Every night, he screamed and flailed out of biological terror as he was put into his crate.

The enclosures in the Duhok Zoo were better than many others I saw in the region, but they were still incredibly small, with cement floors and a lack of any stimulation for the animals. I didn't want to see Manno spend the rest of his life in a small concrete cage.

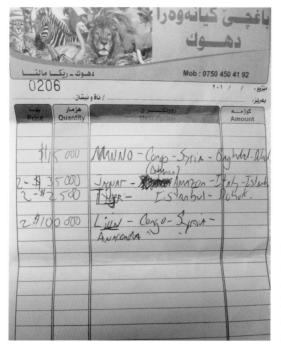

The list of how much each animal in the Duhok Zoo cost helped me realize just how extensive the smuggling market for exotic animals really was.

Dr. Sulaiman Tameer was the founder of KOARP, the Kurdistan Organization for Animal Rights Protection. A one-man veterinary clinic, he taught me about the plight of animals in Kurdistan and was an incredible help in getting Manno out of the Duhok Zoo.

If Manno knew how to do one thing, it was how to get into trouble. I knew that what started as funny antics as a young chimp could quickly become dangerous when he was older and stronger. It was in everyone's best interest to get Manno into a better situation.

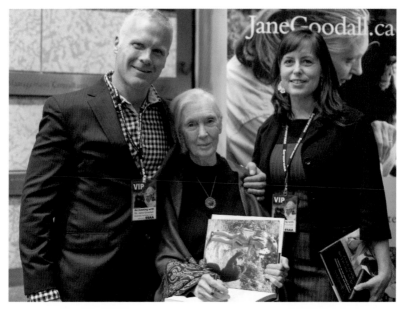

Meeting Jane Goodall was an immense honor. I spent hours rehearsing what I would say when I finally met her, and I was overjoyed when her organization agreed to help with Manno's rescue. *Jane Goodall Institute*

Jason (*left*) and Maggie (*second from left*) were the husband-and-wife team behind Animals Lebanon. We were in constant contact in the months leading up to Manno's rescue as they handled everything on the ground in Kurdistan. When it finally came time to get Manno out, Owen (*right*), a photojournalist contracted by the CBC, was there to document our efforts. *Maggie Shaarawi*

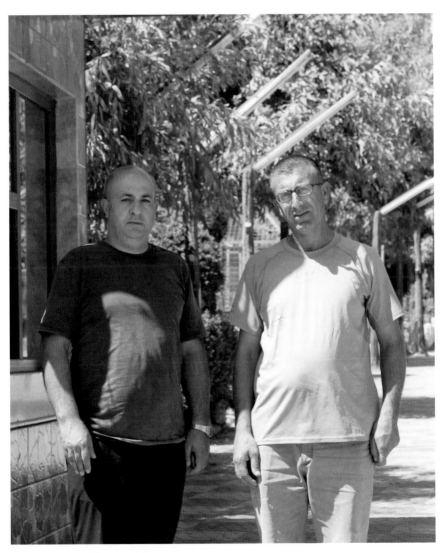

Abdulqadir (*right*) was Manno's caretaker at the Duhok Zoo, which was run by Ramadan (*left*). Abdulqadir and his family loved Manno dearly—Manno even lived in their apartment. Although they knew that Manno couldn't stay with them forever, saying goodbye to him was like saying farewell to a family member.

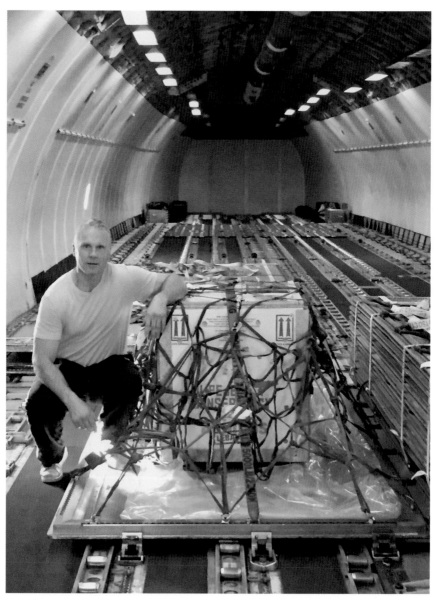

The trip from the Duhok Zoo in Iraqi Kurdistan to Ol Pejeta Conservatory was more than six thousand kilometers. It involved navigating dozens of checkpoints, traveling through an active war zone, and dealing with countless levels of government bureaucracies. But nothing was going to stop us from getting Manno to safety.

Manno's journey didn't end when he arrived at Ol Pejeta Conservatory. He'd spent so long around humans that he had to learn how to be a chimp again. And if he couldn't form a bond with the females of the tribe—who would protect him from the alpha—there was little hope for him there. *Daina Liepa*

Sudan was the last male northern white rhino left in the world when he died in early 2018. He spent his final years at the Ol Pejeta Conservatory, where we brought Manno. Seeing him up close was a humbling reminder of how interconnected all living things are on this planet and how we lost yet another species on our watch. *Samuel Mbogo*

Christie and I told ourselves that we'd wait until Anders was five before getting another dog, but as soon as we met Tux, we knew he had to be a part of our family. My hope is that I can show Anders that every life on this planet is precious. *Chalice Stewart Photography*

This is Manno and me at the end of his quarantine period in Ol Pejeta Conservatory. Although it was bittersweet as it meant I was saying goodbye to my friend and holding him for the last time, I was also happy knowing that we were giving him a chance at a new life. *Alicia Melis*

When Manno was adopted by the female chimps into their tribe at Ol Pejeta Sanctuary, it was a sign that all our hopes had come true. Manno was finally safe. *Daina Liepa*

In February 2016, when Ramadan agreed to release Manno, Jason returned to Iraq to do a run-through of the whole process. He was incredibly meticulous, ensuring that Manno's transfer crate was durable, that there was a truck available that could fit the crate, and that we had a driver willing to transport such precious cargo from Duhok to Erbil. Jason met with cargo agents, airline staff, and politicians. He set up a blood and feces test for Manno to send back to the sanctuary, proving he wasn't a public-health risk. And he met with Ramadan Salim, two years after trying to confiscate Manno the first time. This time, Jason approached Ramadan as humbly as possible, as though it was a request, even though taking Manno was now a government mandate.

Ramadan still had seven more months with Manno while Iraqi officials navigated the new CITES agreement that they'd signed less than two years prior. We remained patient while officials in Iraq and Kenya disputed who was supposed to issue which permits, and which ones needed to be signed and by whom. It was truly unprecedented for Kurdistan, an achievement made all the more remarkable given that it was in the thick of another civil war.

I was lucky enough to get some media attention to help us hold the Kurdish officials to their promises. An excellent CBC journalist, Andrea Huncar, was on the story right from the beginning, too. At the same time, I made sure to regularly broadcast updates of my own online and served as a go-between for the media in Canada and the people on the ground in the Middle East—we all wanted to make sure that Manno remained in the spotlight so that he didn't disappear back onto the black market.

My phone and computer received a constant stream of messages. I continued to receive weekly, if not daily, updates from Sulaiman Tameer in Duhok. He had been regularly checking up on Manno, making sure he was still at the zoo and doing well. Jason also kept me up-to-date on the incredibly sluggish process of securing proper documentation and medical tests. It was agonizingly slow, but the simple

fact that there was near-daily traction assured me this was going to finally happen.

Three years had passed since I'd first met Manno, and though I had never given up hope, there had been many, many moments of doubt. Joy fluttered through my stomach whenever I imagined Manno swinging and playing free with other chimpanzees. When I began my venture, I had hoped that maybe an accredited zoo might take Manno—some place safe, even if it wasn't the most exciting. Never in my wildest dreams could I have imagined that we would find him what he truly deserved: a home.

3: Lessons from Manno

NOVEMBER 2015

Chapter ten

"From what we get, we can make a living; what we give, however, makes a life."

—ARTHUR ASHE, PROFESSIONAL
TENNIS PLAYER

When I arrived in Erbil in late November 2016, almost three years to the month since I met Manno, fully one-third of Iraq had been seized by ISIS. The barbarism of the group had poured over the western border with Syria down a sliver of the central region of Iraq to within miles of Baghdad, and then through a chunk of the north, including Mosul on the Kurdistan border. But the tides were shifting and Iraqi police and military, along with Peshmerga soldiers, were recapturing the country from ISIS one city at a time.

With the Iraqi army preparing to retake Mosul, just eighty-five kilometers from where I stood in the Erbil airport's baggage claim, I wondered if I should hail a taxi to the hotel or to the departures gate.

The atmosphere in the airport was different from what I'd experienced on my first trip, and it was more than just a palpable sense of tension. There was an eerie quiet at the arrivals gate and even fewer flights on the board than there had been when I'd arrived in 2013. And this time, there were more Caucasians waiting for the conveyer belt to spit out bags, many of them with

a military air to them—broad shoulders, straight jaws, tattooed arms and legs.

I said hello to one guy, standing silently on my right, his gaze firmly focused on the rubber flaps of the luggage conveyor belt. He sized me up and nodded.

"Are you with private?" I asked, using the term for ex-military mercenaries doing work in various conflict zones.

"Triple Canopy," he said. "And you?"

I shook my head no. "Freelance," I said with a smile. He raised a brow, intrigued. "I'm helping rescue a chimp." He stared at me, mining for sarcasm, unsure whether to snort or laugh at me.

The baggage claim machine came to life, faintly clinking and puttering, until the steel conveyer belt was gliding clockwise. "Good luck, buddy," he said, grabbing his bag and turning toward the rubber flaps again.

I took my luggage outside and caught a cab to the Rotana Hotel, a striking sight at dusk, glittering blue against an orange sky, with tropical trees around the eleven-story building. The opulent entrance was hidden behind heavy iron fencing lined by a cement barricade. Before the young guards opened the gate, they used telescoping mirrors to inspect the cab's undercarriage for explosives and weapons, and brought over a dog to sniff the vehicle. Finally, they stepped aside, opened the gate, and waved us in.

Considered the best place to stay in Iraq, the five-star Rotana hosted diplomats and billionaires, treating them to almost embarrassingly lavish service from the moment they entered the airy foyer and checked in at the expansive onyx front desk manned by staff in ash-colored suits with embroidered collars. One of Jason's donors had worked out a deal with the posh hotel to take care of us. Still, I felt immediately underdressed in my cargo pants and corduroy jacket.

I checked into my room and waited for Jason to arrive on his flight from Beirut. He called me from his room a couple hours later

and asked me to meet him for dinner. I found him in the hotel restaurant with Maggie Shaarawi, his partner in Animals Lebanon and in life—the other reason this American farm boy had uprooted himself to live in Beirut.

Over dinner, I asked question after question about Jason's previous rescues. He told me horrific stories about rescuing baby tigers abandoned at airports in sketchy crates, as well as more relatable stories about helping find homes for street dogs and cats. Their apartment in Beirut was a foster home for kittens who arrived scraggly and malnourished and left healthy and friendly, with happy new owners.

"My job," Jason said, "is to help all animals nationally, as best we can. We don't focus on a species or even a type of animal."

One thing was apparent though: chimps were his imperative—his main driver that got him into the field and kept him there.

"What is it about them?" I asked.

"You will see Jason is happiest when he is with a chimpanzee," Maggie said in her musical Lebanese accent.

Jason grinned and brushed his hair back behind his ears. "From 2000 until now, my life's been defined by working with them," he said. "I've been to so many countries, met so many people, had so many experiences, all because of trying to help chimps. But in the end, it's just nice to help something that needs help, and I just think it's an animal worth saving."

Jason articulated perfectly what had been simmering in my thoughts for years. I had tremendous respect for him and the fact that he devoted his entire adult life to what I had just dipped my big toe into.

The next morning, an adviser to the prime minister's office, along with a cargo agent and an Emirates airline representative, met us in the hotel restaurant for breakfast. A video journalist living in Erbil whom the CBC hired was there, too. The airline representative proudly talked up the cargo infrastructure and how many

exotic animals they'd transported, which unsettled me, but I'd be lying if I said it didn't also reassure me that Manno would get to Kenya safely. The adviser also assured us that Ramadan was willing to give Manno up without any issues. Everything felt set to run smoothly.

"That was much more encouraging than the last time I met with government officials" about Manno, Jason confided in me after the others had left. It went to show that if you wanted to get things done, sometimes you needed to bypass all the middlemen and go right to the top.

Still, even without intentional meddling, what can go wrong sometimes will go wrong. The first sign of that universal law at work arrived in the form of the SUV meant to transport the custom crate Jason built for Manno, a wooden box reinforced with steel edges and smooth, white plastic siding, and decorated with Animals Lebanon and Ol Pejeta's logos. It was not the vehicle Jason had arranged for after his trial run back in winter. He'd asked for a Suburban, and we were sent a Jeep. The difference? About 1.5 centimeters of trunk storage. We tried repeatedly to fit the crate into the back of the new car. We flipped the crate on its side. We wiggled and shimmied it. Tried to push it corner-first. But nothing worked. After forty-five minutes we gave up and sent back our ride.

By the time another sport-utility vehicle arrived, we'd lost an hour. It didn't seem like much, but we had little time to spare. There were so many players along the route—if just one of them decided that we'd missed our window, the whole thing could fall apart. Worse, with brutal Islamic extremists warring too close for comfort and suicide bombings becoming increasingly frequent in Kurdistan, I couldn't tell how long the region would remain quiet enough to transport Manno safely.

I popped open the hatch, peered into the back of the SUV, and turned back to Jason with an uneasy grin. "It doesn't look much bigger than the last truck."

"It'll work," he said, grabbing a side of the crate.

I grabbed the other end and we hauled the crate onto the tailgate. Tilted fifteen degrees, it slid through like a blade in a knife block, scraping the sides of the plastic interior, but fitting nonetheless. I pumped my fist and threw my arm around Jason's shoulders. He clamped up. "Uh, I'm not much of a hugger," he said, offering a fist bump.

We crammed into the car—me, Jason, Maggie, the video journalist, and our hired driver—and set out on the drive to Duhok. We took a zigzagging, detour route through barren rolling hills so that we could avoid the Mosul battles as best we could. Still, the road would come within kilometers of Mosul, where a military coalition was trying to retake one of ISIS's last strongholds. The terrifying reality was that ISIS would not go down without a fight and their desperation was chilling. With extreme violence only a few dozen kilometers away, we crossed many Kurdish checkpoints, and we knew there was an ever-present danger of roadside attacks, mined roads, and VBIEDs.

I sat beside the journalist on the drive out, and it quickly became clear that this assignment was a respite for him. For the past few years, he'd been embedded with armies and rebel groups in Mosul and Fallujah, and he'd seen his fair share of violence. "I've noticed a lot of dead human feet lately," he said. "Here, I'll show you."

"No, thank you," I said before he could pull out his phone.

I tried to relax, maybe even enjoy the scenic drive on this bright warm day. The crimson fields, the mountain peaks dusted in snow, the glistening Tigris River—it had all appeared so beautiful to me on my first trip. But, with every hill we rolled over and every bend we took, my fears kept hijacking the scenery with visions of a truck loaded with masked men pumping Kalashnikovs in the air and approaching from afar.

"How safe is this road?" I asked the driver, who knew the area.

"The Battle of Mosul certainly doesn't make this easier," he said. "We've tried to minimize the number of people who know about our

movement. But there's not much we can do about it. We just need to accept it and focus on our task."

The driver pulled into a gas station to refuel. I opened the maps app on my phone. There was just a twenty-five-kilometer buffer between us and ISIS fighters. The driver popped the gas cap back on and paid, then lit a cigarette in the shade. *If he's comfortable enough for a smoke break here, then maybe I should ease up*, I thought.

The driver returned to the wheel and turned the keys in the ignition.

Click click click click click click click.

He twisted the keys back, then turned them forward. The dashboard gauge lights flickered red.

Click click click click click click click.

The driver turned around, looking over his shoulder with the calmness of someone asking for a glass of water. "We need a push."

Maggie, Jason, and I exchanged wide eyes. "You're kidding?" I said. He was not. I took a deep breath, then stepped outside into the filling station lot and propped myself behind the SUV with the other passengers.

The initial big push got the vehicle rolling, ever so slowly. We tried to avoid tripping over potholes as the truck's momentum picked up. Finally, as the truck gained speed, we heard the triumphant sound of the ignition firing up. The driver smiled as we all piled back in, but I was starting to doubt whether those wheels were up to the task of moving Manno and keeping us safe.

When we finally got to Duhok, hours late, we headed straight to the Ministry of Agriculture office to meet the government representative mediating Manno's confiscation. When we entered the meeting room, I was shocked to find none other than Sulaiman Tameer.

"My friend!" Sulaiman exclaimed, pulling me in for many cheek kisses and a hug. "Thank God you arrive safely."

When he let go, I noticed something different about him. *Is he slimmer? His complexion fuller?* "Sulaiman, buddy, you look great."

"Yes, my friend," he said. "I quit smoking. Two years now. I'll tell you why—we have a new baby and her father, he needs to be healthy."

"Proud of you, buddy," I said, slapping his back. I reached into my pocket and pulled out my phone to show him the picture of Anders on my lock screen.

"*Subhanallah,*" he gasped. "It is Little Spencer. I would never have believed it."

"Me neither, but you were right—children *are* the vegetables of the home."

I introduced Sulaiman to Jason and Maggie. There was an unusual air about their handshake, as though they were trying to place each other.

"I think . . ." Sulaiman said.

"Yes," Jason agreed. "We have."

"But where?"

"Was it?"

"I cannot exactly remember."

Finally Maggie chimed in: "It was the Egypt conference." They erupted with excitement as they remembered their first meeting. After a bumpy morning, it was shaping up to be a nice reunion.

There was still lots to be done. Sulaiman beckoned us to follow him—I figured we were heading to collect Manno's release forms or other official documents. Instead, Sulaiman led us to a table full of coffee, tea, and fruit. *When in Kurdistan,* I thought, smiling at the thought that, even in the midst of such upheaval, hospitality trumped all.

Finally, we got down to business and went over the plan.

"We will arrive at the Duhok Zoo, as Ramadan Salim is expecting us, and hopefully he'll remain courteous," Jason said. "No matter what, we are to remain respectful and thankful for his cooperation."

"We want to reinforce the positive outcomes of bringing Manno to a sanctuary," Maggie added. "Jason will remind Ramadan that his organization is well connected with world-class biologists and zoos around the world, and he's willing to offer support if he'd like it."

"Like what?" I asked.

"Ramadan's zoo has a number of animals without the best care," Jason said, recalling what he saw on his last visit. "We can offer vaccinations and help improve the quality of care and feeding schedules for animals, so long as he's willing to commit to stopping some negative things."

I marveled at how a tiny organization such as Jason's—one whose agenda was unpopular with many people—could wield so much influence. It all came down to his approach, disarming with positivity and making people feel as though they are part of a greater cause, even if they started on the opposite side of it.

As we left the room, I asked Jason, "How do you feel about our chances?"

"We have everything in place," he said. "But I'll admit, I'm still a bit worried that things could go sideways. If Ramadan has a change of heart, he could put Manno into hiding at any time."

I recognized the danger. A second failed attempt at releasing Manno might be enough to convince the Kurdish government and cooperating parties that this chimpanzee simply wasn't worth the hassle. With that in mind, we returned to the SUV and set out to Duhok Zoo to rescue Manno before it was too late.

When we got to the zoo, I waited outside the artificial stone entrance with Jason and Maggie while Sulaiman went in search of Ramadan to make sure everything was in order. The zoo had been upgraded and expanded greatly since my last visit. A new water feature was so loud it drowned out the voices of families entering the front gate. As the minutes passed, I could feel the heat from the sun on my bare arms intensify. It was December, but compared to the winter back home, we were in the midst a heat wave, and the

power of the sun, even in winter, was intense. Jason had obviously acclimatized to winters in the Middle East differently, wearing a heavy black hoodie and betraying no discomfort under the beaming sun.

Finally, Sulaiman, wearing an even heavier suit jacket, returned with his hands in his pockets. *Oh no, something's gone wrong,* I thought when I saw his posture.

"Everything okay?" I asked.

"Yes, Manno is here. They will bring him out now."

I craned my neck, looking past his shoulder, waiting to see Manno. I spotted a couple of figures walking toward us. At first, it appeared to be a man carrying a big child in his arms. As they got closer, though, I realized the kid in a red-and-white baseball shirt and rainbow pants was my old friend.

Manno had his whole body wrapped around the man. My hands instinctively stretched toward Manno, expecting him to leap into my embrace the moment he was near enough. But instead, Manno looked away, keeping his grip on the guy. My arms dropped. It was immediately clear: I wasn't Manno's entire world anymore.

Stroking his head until he finally looked at me, I asked, "Do you remember me?" I knew it was unrealistic to think Manno would immediately remember me, but still, I couldn't help but hope. Physically, I had to search for familiarity in his features. By now, Manno was almost four and closer to maturity. His round facial features were flattening out as his face elongated. His limbs were getting more muscular. His black hair thickening and spreading.

He seemed unreceptive to my petting and voice, as did his caretaker, Abdulqadir Ghalab Abdi, who was understandably cold to me. A Syrian refugee, Abdulqadir worked at the zoo but was paid extra to take Manno home and care for him after closing. He wore a sweater with rolled up sleeves, and his gaunt face was stubbled with salt-and-pepper hair, a pair of rectangular glasses sitting slightly askew on his nose. He and Manno locked eyes, and it was

crystal clear that they'd bonded deeply over the last years. I tried to put myself in the caretaker's shoes, wondering how it would feel to be separated from a friend, even if it was for that friend's own good.

Suddenly, Jason, standing behind me, puckered his lips and began hooting and panting. Manno instantly perked up and stretched in Jason's direction, forcing Abdulqadir to let him down on the pavement. Jason crouched down to Manno's eye level and they spoke chimp to one another, then embraced. Jason gestured for me to approach Manno, now that he'd been comforted and felt like he could trust our company. Manno sat on the ground and I squatted beside him, rubbing and scratching his back and kissing his head, which was sparsely covered with long, black wiry hair. Finally, Manno let me lift him into my arms and we hugged.

He stayed in my arms, clutching me, as I carried him into the marble-tiled office where Ramadan had first scribbled the smuggling routes and market prices for his animals that became my main piece of evidence in rescuing Manno. Ramadan was waiting for us now, wearing a black sweater. Though he wasn't in any way acting hostile toward us, there was an iciness to the man who had once called me his brother. *He must feel like I've betrayed him*, I thought. The conditions of Manno's release had no doubt upset him. Every request Ramadan had made in exchange for Manno— money, new animals, maybe a couple of cheetahs—had only been met with offers of better training and equipment, which didn't interest him at all.

Yet, despite his loss, Ramadan's Middle Eastern manners of extreme hospitality were intact. He poured coffee and distributed water bottles to us all. He gave me a bag of sunflower seeds to feed to Manno. I was surprised to see that, whereas before Manno had melted in my arms when I held him, now he munched the heap of seeds in my hand with force and restlessness. Sitting beside me, Abdulqadir smiled at Manno wistfully, praising the chimpanzee in Arabic to Maggie. He

cared deeply for Manno, as did the zookeepers pouring in and out of the office to say their goodbyes. They obviously loved him as much as any human can love an animal. It saddened me to separate Manno from these people who cared so much for him, but I was resolute that we were doing the right thing. Manno was so much bigger and stronger, and yet still a juvenile. He needed to be in a safe place. For Manno's sake, as well as for their own.

While Sulaiman and Ramadan finalized the release forms, Manno enjoyed the attention from all his human friends and admirers, as well as the camera filming his last moments at the zoo. I wasn't sure what was being communicated in Kurdish between Sulaiman and Ramadan, but Ramadan's mood gradually started to change. He became warmer to everyone and even started smiling at Manno, who panted gleefully and basked in the spotlight. *Is it just the dozens of stroking hands against his fur that are delighting him?* I wondered. *Or does he sense something new and special waiting for him?*

Abdulqadir was sniffling and trying to conceal his hurt, but his red wet eyes betrayed the gap-toothed smile he tried to give Manno. I put a comforting hand on his shoulder, thanked him for being a great caretaker and friend to Manno. He responded in Arabic, and I turned to Maggie to translate for us.

"How are you feeling?" I asked through Maggie.

"I feel like I am giving up a liver," she translated back.

"I can tell that he loves you."

Abdulqadir nodded vigorously. "He likes to do everything with me—sleep on the floor with me, take a shower, watch football. He brings me water or the remote control for the TV."

"And I can tell you love him."

"He is like my son. We have four children, they all love him, and Manno is like a fifth child. He spends time with the family and eats rice and pita, just like us. I change his diapers."

"Is he a lot of work?"

"He is rambunctious, but he wouldn't hurt anyone. We have a

four-month-old baby, and when she cries, Manno hugs her. We teach him to be good. But if someone hurts our children, or if our children hurt each other, Manno will yell and protect them if he thinks they are in trouble."

It sounded sweet, but it was an unsettling thought. How could Manno properly decipher between threatening situations and, say, horseplay? Intelligent a being as he was, he spoke another language, and no matter how well his caretakers could imitate it, something was always bound to be lost in translation.

"Do you know what a sanctuary is?"

"Yes."

"And are you okay with him going there?"

"I know Manno will be better there than here."

Manno crawled from my lap into Abdulqadir's, embraced him tenderly, and pressed his face against the man's chest. As Abdulqadir stroked Manno's lips and pinched his chin, he began to weep uncontrollably. I was also fighting back tears. Here was a man whose life had been upturned by war, who had to leave everyone and everything behind in Syria, but managed to scrape together a sense of peace and stability for his family. And along the way, he found unexpected joy in the same sweet creature who'd changed my life, too.

He said something to Maggie, who relayed back to us: "He says he would like his children to say goodbye to Manno."

I looked around at Jason and Maggie. "Do we have time?" I asked.

"Of course," Jason said.

"Where does he live?"

It wasn't far, but there were other matters to attend to first. I was eager to get going as quickly as possible so that we weren't driving at night, but in typical Kurdish fashion, Ramadan and Sulaiman insisted on having lunch together. Knowing how long a Kurdish lunch lasts, my first thought was, *No way! Let's get out of here.* But Jason, in his wisdom, calmly said, "Yes, let's feast." He gave me a look, as if to say,

Remain respectful. Ramadan took us to the zoo restaurant, where we were served a cavalcade of warm naan, spiced rice, kebabs, hummus, and tzatziki. I could hardly get out of my chair by the time the table was cleared.

After lunch, we followed Abdulqadir a couple hundred feet—we hadn't even left the zoo grounds when we arrived at the three-story building. Abdulqadir's family lived in a small suite in the corner of the compound, where Ramadan had generously allowed them to live for three years. Seeing Ramadan's quiet compassion, I could tell that when it came down to it, he was motivated by the heart more than money.

It was a humble living arrangement: a bathroom, kitchen, living room, and bedroom shared between six—seven including Manno. Abdulqadir's wife, wearing a floral hijab, lit up and said a prayer upon seeing Manno. She charged over and kissed the chimp repeatedly, then just as quickly did a head count of her guests—me, Jason, Maggie, Sulaiman, Ramadan, and the photojournalist—and started preparing six cups of Turkish coffee.

Sulaiman tapped the shoulder of our photographer, who was pointing his camera in the kitchen. "No pictures of the women, please," Sulaiman advised.

We took our shoes off and got comfortable in the living room, the floor layered with cushions and blankets. The youngest child was a babbling baby, sitting upright against a throw pillow and gnawing on the end of the remote control. Once his feet were on the ground, Manno immediately scooted toward the baby, and she nuzzled against him. They squealed at each other, nothing but delight and playfulness. On one hand, it was a beautiful example of interspecies connectedness, and how humanlike chimps really are. But it was also sobering to know how quickly this exchange could turn tragic.

The sweet baby had no idea that this was the last she would see of her friend, but her siblings were wailing. They'd already prepared for Manno to go, and seeing him once more, though a thoughtful gesture,

had driven up their hopes that something would change. When they realized this was just one more sad goodbye, they broke down. Abdul-qadir's six-year-old begged Ramadan not to take Manno away, pulling Ramadan's pant leg, saying, "*Raja, Ammo, raja*" ("Please, Uncle, please").

Abdulqadir stepped toward her with a gentle hand on her shoulder. "*Ya, baba*," he said, wiping her tears with the same hand with which he wiped his own. He gestured for his other two children to huddle close to him and quietly explained the situation.

"What's Abdulqadir saying?" I asked Maggie.

"He is telling them that Manno does not belong to any of us—he belongs to the world. Manno cannot stay here and get older, because once he is older he'll be too strong to keep inside. He has to go back home to Africa."

The sentiment was true, and my heart swelled at the poetry of his words. As Abdulqadir explained the world awaiting Manno to his children, their tears began to dry and they began to laugh.

Maggie continued, "He is telling them that it will be better for Manno to be with other chimpanzees. Maybe he will find a girlfriend and she will protect him and take care of him." Maggie paused and smiled. "Ramadan says that Manno is getting married in Africa."

"If he doesn't get married," his daughter said, "send him back."

Everyone sipped tea and gave the family their final moments with Manno. Eventually, Jason tapped his watch and quietly let Abdulqadir know that we needed to get back on schedule. Abdulqadir broke the news to his kids as softly as he could, but it didn't stop a torrent of tears and begging for more time. I knew the children couldn't fully grasp why this was happening, but I also knew it was for the best, and I prayed that one day they would see pictures of Manno thriving in the sanctuary, with his "wife" (or wives), and feel the same way. As we walked away, my heart broke at the sound of their uncontrollable wailing. Manno had touched my heart after caring for him for a few weeks. I couldn't imagine losing him after living with him for years.

Back at the entrance of the zoo, the big wood crate that Jason and Maggie built for Manno sat in the parking lot, the metal-bar door opening to a comfortable bed of shredded paper. We tried to guide Manno into it, but he wasn't having it. He splayed his limbs to all four edges of the crate and clutched tightly, bracing his body with all his might. He'd spent too much time in cages before Abdulqadir's family took him in to crawl into another box now.

Jason unzipped a black pouch and took out a plunger with a clear liquid in it. The sight of it triggered my memories of putting down Mac, Emma, and Chloe over such a short time, one lethal dosage after another, and I instinctively objected.

"It's just to calm him down," Jason explained. "It won't put him out in any sense. He's just upset by the sight of the crate." He sat on a rocky ledge by the water feature, holding the plunger in one hand and, with the other, tried to open Manno's mouth by touching his lips. But Manno was skeptical and stubbornly refused to unclench his jaw.

Abdulqadir lifted Manno into his arms and hugged him, then offered to administer the syringe to him. Jason handed Abdulqadir the clear plunger. Abdulqadir showed it to Manno, revealing, I presume, that there was nothing sharp or threatening to it. He gently touched Manno's lips with the tip of it, and Manno's mouth opened, his puckered lips slurping the fluid out of the end.

We gave the sedative a half hour for the effects to take. I played with and hugged Manno to try and calm him down, but aside from making Manno more affectionate, the sedative didn't change his opinion on the crate. *Box bad*, he seemed to tell us, shaking his head as Jason tried to coax him into it.

"He's actively resisting," Jason said. "We can't force it. We don't want him to have a negative association." He was right. If Manno was going to spend the better part of the next two days in a box, we had to make sure that box was a place he wanted to be in. But no matter how many fruits we placed in it or how gently we tried to nudge him in, he

wouldn't budge. The closest he'd get was a foot from the opening, at which point, he'd flop belly up on the pavement.

Then Abdulqadir had an idea. He picked up a black bag of garbage waiting for disposal by the curb and said something to Ramadan in Arabic. He headed over to the utility shed and returned with just the big black plastic garbage bag flowing in the breeze. *Does he seriously want to put Manno in a bag?*

Abdulqadir placed the trash bag on the pavement and, like magic, Manno ambled over to it on his knuckles and feet and lay on it quietly. *Now what?*

Abdulqadir nodded at Jason to follow his lead. He pinched the corners of the bag and Jason did the same on the other side, then they hoisted Manno up like a body on a stretcher and carried him to the crate. They gently inserted him—bag and all—into the box. Jason pulled the bag away a bit, revealing Manno, who grinned at us through his curled-up lips and immediately went about making a nest in the shredded paper. Obviously, he'd been trained to sit on garbage bags, for what reason I'd never know.

Jason and Maggie secured the crate's bars and bolted it shut, allowing Manno to sleep off the rest of the tranquilizer. I helped Jason load Manno into the back of the SUV and gently shut the trunk door. Then, I turned to say the first of many goodbyes on that trip. Sulaiman was staying behind in Duhok. I gave him a big hug, and then shared the same with Abdulqadir. Finally, I came to Ramadan. I offered my hand, but to my surprise, he pulled me in for the customary three cheek kisses, then waved goodbye as I hopped into the passenger seat.

Catching Sulaiman's eye, I asked him to translate something into Kurdish for me. "Please, tell Ramadan that I say thank you for giving Manno a second chance."

Ramadan nodded back warmly as Sulaiman relayed my message.

Three years ago, I'd made a pledge to get Manno to a sanctuary. I couldn't believe we'd come this far. Manno was securely in

our custody and we were leaving the zoo on the best terms possible. But, like climbing Kilimanjaro, getting to the top of the mountain is merely an option—it's getting down that's nonnegotiable. And we still had a long way to go on our six-thousand-kilometer downhill stretch to Kenya.

Chapter eleven

"The battle line between good and evil runs through the heart of every man."

—ALEKSANDR SOLZHENITSYN,
NOVELIST AND HISTORIAN

About thirty minutes after we left the Duhok Zoo, we were about to pass within a few kilometers of perhaps the most ferocious battle currently being waged in the world. Just when I'd started relaxing and taking in the sun disappearing behind desert mountains, Jason suddenly exclaimed, "Oh, no!"

"What is it?" asked Maggie.

"I forgot the release papers in Ramadan's office."

The driver pulled a U-turn and we headed back to the zoo. Thankfully, Ramadan had the papers waiting for us and we were back on track soon. Still, I couldn't help but wonder if it was an omen of things to come.

It was a good thing we turned back, though, because it wasn't just the release papers we had to recover. Jason forgot his phone in Ramadan's office, too. "He's not very good with phones," Maggie said, laughing, as we pulled out of the Duhok Zoo for the second time that day.

Once we were back on the road, Jason checked his phone and saw that there were a bunch of missed calls from an Emirates airline

representative. Sitting in the back, one arm hanging over the seat so Manno could feel my hand through the bars, I paid close attention to Jason in the passenger seat. Night had settled around us, and the only physical part of him I could make out was his frown glowing in the light of his cell phone.

"I'm sorry, what do you mean? . . . Pardon me. . . . Why?" he said to the caller.

Until that moment, Jason had been utterly calm, but for the first time I was detecting unease in his voice.

"What's going on?" Maggie asked quietly during a pause in the conversation.

"They say Manno can't go on the cargo plane," Jason whispered.

"Why not?" I exclaimed.

Jason held up his hand to cool me, then, into the phone, said, "I will call you right back, okay? Sorry for the confusion. . . . No, I won't be long." He hung up and immediately started texting vigorously. As he punched the keys, he explained, "It appears that nobody has paid for Manno's cargo ticket."

"Who are you texting?" I asked.

"Our contact at the sanctuary."

"Why?"

"Because they were supposed to pay for his cargo ticket," Jason said, sending off the text with a final push and slamming the phone on the dashboard, where it sat silently for a long time.

Finally, it pinged. Jason snatched it up and looked at the screen. He was about to text back, but then shook his head and called instead. After only a few seconds, he hung up and redialed. Then again. Either the spotty cell reception in the Kenyan wild and the Kurdish mountains meant his calls weren't going through, or someone didn't want to talk to us.

Jason turned around, his face racked with exasperation.

"We sorted out Manno's flight with the understanding that our contact at the sanctuary would wire money to the cargo agency," he

said. "Now the airline is saying that didn't happen and nothing's been done to secure Manno's spot on the plane."

We'd worked on this plan meticulously for three years, so for things to be put aside until the last minute like this left us all feeling incredibly frustrated. Maggie and I tried to keep Jason optimistic, but in our deeply fatigued state, winding through these dangerous roads in total darkness, we didn't sound very convincing. We all had our own flights booked tomorrow—me back to Canada, Jason and Maggie to Lebanon—except Manno. Apparently, he wasn't going anywhere.

We spent the rest of the ride trying to figure out a new plan. All of our partners—the airline, the sanctuary, the cargo company—had Jason's number, so his phone was pinging nonstop as we tried to buy time with the airline.

"If we can't get him out today, when's the next cargo plane?" I asked.

A series of texts. Then Jason said, "Not for another week."

I thought about it. War was still going on around us. If he was stuck in the middle of it for a week with no one to watch over him, who knows what might happen. The last thing I wanted was for Manno to be stuck in limbo or slip through the cracks.

"I will stay behind," I said.

Jason gave me a look. "I don't want you to have to do that," he said.

"I want us all to get home safely, but . . ." I hesitated, thinking of the logistics. "Look, we've worked far too hard to get us to this point. There's nothing that I won't do to get Manno safely to Sweetwaters. I'm all in."

In a last-ditch effort, Jason decided to call Sulaiman to see if the Kurdish government could do something—anything—to get Manno on the plane the next day. He asked the driver to pull over by a road-side market for better reception.

While Jason made the call, I wandered over to the table of produce and bought mangos and dried fruit from two young boys. They

sat under a canopy that shook in the wind, watching the trucks zoom by. "*Spas*" ("Thank you"), I said, unrolling a couple extra hundred dinars and placing a bill in each boy's hands.

Lit up by our SUV's headlights, Jason paced in front of the car with his hands in his pockets. When his phone rang, he tore his hand out of his pocket and pressed it to his ear. I got inside the car with Maggie and slipped Manno the fruit through the bars. As Manno ripped into a mango, I quietly said to him, "I know I promised you we'd get you out of here. We might need a little more time, but my promise stands, little man."

Suddenly, the passenger door opened. Jason sat quietly, saying nothing.

"Well?" Maggie asked.

"That was Emirates airline," he said, then looked up with a smile. "We've got a spot for Manno."

The caravan exploded with cheering. Manno, excited by the noise, contributed with his own shrieking.

"So everything came through with the sanctuary?" I asked.

"Not exactly, but that's not important," said Jason, turning to me. "Spencer, you're going to Africa."

"Are you serious?"

"My job is to get Manno on that cargo plane to Africa, and then my job's done, but we need someone with him along the way. Are you up for it?"

I didn't even think about it. "Of course!" I said. Then my rational brain kicked in. "Jason, who's paying for these flights?"

He smiled, then turned to stare straight ahead at the road in front of him. The driver started the ignition and pulled back onto the highway.

Manno announced his arrival at the five-star hotel with a piercing scream that echoed off the shining marble floors and rattled the

chandelier. The bellboy pushing his transport crate on a luggage cart jumped back. I look around the Rotana Hotel lobby, laughing. The nicest hotel in Iraq was hosting an elaborate wedding, and we'd just crashed it with a wild chimpanzee. The guests, intrigued by Manno's panting and hooting, gathered around him and began fawning and taking pictures. Even the three military contractors in civilian clothes (given away by the molded earpieces and attached cords that disappeared under their shirt collars) slowed their brisk walks to get a good look at the hotel's special guest. Manno somersaulted in his shredded paper and towels, amused by the attention he was gathering. *There's the boy I met three years ago.*

"What is his name?" asked a young man in a tuxedo.

"Manno," I said.

The young man broke into uncontrollable laughter. "Manno? That's my brother's name!"

The bellboy returned from the SUV with our other bags and set them on another cart. I left my things and wheeled Manno's cart to the elevator to take him downstairs. Jason, Maggie, and I had regular rooms, but Manno would have to stay in the utility room, we'd been told. I was planning on sleeping next to him on a fold-out cot.

"Excuse me, Mr. Spencer?" asked a hotel attendant. She handed me a key card in a little envelope. "I hope he enjoys his stay with us." I flipped open the envelope. She'd written "Mr. Manno" on the inside. The hotel had generously allowed Manno to stay with me in my room on the fifth floor, next to Jason and Maggie's.

We laughed about it as we stepped inside the glass elevator. The three of us and Manno squeezed in with the bellboy, who brought Manno's dolly right to his room. Inside, a silver platter of vegetables and fruit awaited him. Pineapple, passion fruit, kiwi—heaps of exotic foods he'd likely never had before.

For the last three years, Manno had been a captive zoo attraction. Now, he was in the luxurious surroundings of Kurdistan's best hotel. Surprisingly, he seemed right at home. No fussing, no crying,

no shrieking. He let us tickle him, which he loved, and feed him food, which he loved more. After his meal, he played in his shredded paper, moving piles from one side of the crate to the other. He somersaulted over to the crate door and pressed his back against it, daring us to tickle him again. I obliged, and he burst into panting laughter. The Manno I remembered was back.

The hotel phone rang and I answered it. It was the front desk, saying we had a visitor.

"It's a high government official," was all the concierge would say.

"Please send them up," I said. I relayed the message to Jason and Maggie, then rushed to the bathroom with my luggage to change into a dress shirt and tie.

I was trying to press the creases out of my shirt when someone knocked on the door. A burly, mustached security detail was on the other side—apparently he needed to scope out the room to make sure it was clear and safe for our visitor. After walking around the perimeter of the room, looking behind the closet and bathroom doors, and checking the drapes, he peered behind Manno's crate. Finally, the bodyguard left and returned with the minister of agriculture, a man with a push-broom mustache, wearing a black suit with a crisp white shirt and shiny tie. He entered with the prime minister's personal secretary and another dignitary, while their security left the room and stood guard in the hallway. The minister shook our hands and exchanged a few words with us in English, asking how the meeting with Ramadan went.

"May I meet this Manno?" he asked.

We cleared the way for him and gestured to the crate. The minister sat on the edge of the queen-size bed beside the transport crate and crouched forward to get a good look. Manno, who was the cause of so much diplomacy and negotiation—and surely so much paperwork for this man's department—lay upside down in his paper nest, quietly staring back at the minister with his huge brown eyes.

"So you're the fellow all the fuss is about?" He smiled at Manno. "Can you take him out?" he asked.

Jason, Maggie, and I exchanged looks. We peered around the room, imagining Manno smashing a mirror, tearing apart the paintings on the wall, ripping apart what looked like Egyptian cotton curtains, or, worse, biting a statesman. "We better not," I said, picturing the next day's headlines if my worst fears were realized.

"No problem," said the minister. "May I touch him?"

"Go ahead," Jason said.

As the minister stroked Manno's head, he said, without a drop of irony in his voice, "On behalf of Prime Minister Nechirvan Barzani and the Kurdistan Regional Government, we bid you farewell and good fortune in Africa."

I wondered if *that* was who was paying for our flights the next day.

Manno's star treatment continued in the morning. When we got to the warehouse at the Erbil airport, a steady stream of personnel trickled in through the hangar doors, each of them snapping pictures of the special cargo. Manno lay on his side, calm if not content, as staff took selfies with him, caressed his hand through the bars, whispered to each other about his cuteness, and played a game he loved called "try to grab my finger through the cage." I appreciated how much love Manno was getting, but I took it with a grain of salt—I recognized that the attention reinforced why we humans put such a high price on exotic animals, their status as a commodity to zoo owners and exhibitors, and the lengths smugglers will go to cash in on that demand.

I was thankful we were getting him out now, when he was still a juvenile and able to adapt to the simulated wild he was about to arrive in.

That was the hope, at least. After he arrived at Ol Pejeta Conservancy in Laikipia Plateau, a semiarid plain at the base of Mount Kenya, Manno wouldn't just be released into the sanctuary. He'd have to begin by undergoing medical assessments in quarantine, the first of many steps toward his full integration into the chimpanzee family. His integration hinged on whether the females accepted him into

their tribe. The males surely wouldn't, so if the females also rejected Manno, it would put his life in danger and his future in limbo again.

Right now, however, the most important thing was keeping the environment calm in order to keep his cortisol levels low. Jason gave Manno another sedative to keep him calm for the long flight to Dubai and then on to Nairobi the following day. He stood, and we turned to face each other. It was time for me to part ways with Jason and Maggie, who were going back to their home in Beirut.

"This has been incredible," I said. "Thank you for everything you've done and taught me."

"This is what we do," Jason said matter-of-factly. "I hope we can do something together again."

"Absolutely," I said. "You've changed my life."

Maggie and I exchanged cheek kisses, and Jason put out his hand for a warm handshake that I pushed aside in favor of a warm embrace. He might not have been a hugger, but we were bonded by something much bigger than any embrace, for the rest of our lives.

With Manno ready for the flight and Jason and Maggie gone, I picked up my bag and headed into the airport proper. An airport employee on a motorized cart escorted me past security and drove me onto the tarmac under a cloudless sky. There, I boarded a white windowless MD-11 cargo plane, the words "Global Africa" written in green block letters on the side of the fuselage. I watched as the ground crew rolled Manno's transport crate to the edge of a conveyor belt that stretched up to the side of our jet. A loadmaster climbed up the side of the scaffolding and extended it inside the aircraft. A switch flicked, and Manno began his ascent.

"Chimpanzee, they tell me." I turned to the French-Canadian voice beside me. A tall, gregarious bald man greeted me with a firm handshake. "I'm your captain," he said before I could notice the four gold stripes on his shoulder patch.

"Easier than the rhinos we've moved, that's for sure," he continued. "Hardest one? Dolphins, just last month. There were a bunch of

them out of Japan. They had someone pouring water on them, taking a bucket from one tank to another, the whole ten hours. Thought we were going to lose one." He shook his head. "The Emiratis really love their exotic animals."

"Dubai's just a stopover," I said. "This guy's going back to Africa."

The pilot looked at me and his eyes brightened a little. I gave him a quick rundown about why I was with Manno and where we were taking him. He nodded approvingly throughout.

While the crew took turns greeting their special cargo in his crate, which was securely strapped to the floor of the plane, the pilot invited me into the cockpit for takeoff, teaching me about the various technologies and dos and don'ts of his trade. Once we were in the air, he pointed to a thin line on the digital map. "See that?" he asked. "That's the no-fly zone over Mosul. We stay away from that."

"And if something happens?" I asked.

"See all those locations marked in purple? I can have this plane on the ground in seven minutes flat."

I glanced back into the cargo area, which was like staring through a giant's rib cage. I'd left the crate's door open so I could see Manno through the bars. It was a once-in-a-lifetime experience in the cockpit, but it was a once-in-a-hundred-lifetimes in the back. The international crew from Indonesia, Rhodesia, Finland, and Quebec made their rounds, checking data on a clipboard, measuring the weight of Manno's crate, and physically securing the loads throughout the hold. The pilots went through the battery of checks in the cockpit, not once but twice. Except for a few pallets of cargo, this massive arched cave had one purpose—to get a single primate out of a harm's way. It seemed very cloak-and-dagger, like the animal rescue version of 007, and Manno was none the wiser. He remained calm, playing with the curious crew through his cage, napping or rolling around in the paper in his crate.

Finally, the aircraft descended toward Dubai, its skyscraper lights glowing like candles at sunset. I reached for my camera and snapped

photos as the Burj Khalifa, the tallest building in the world, soared into view, but I quickly turned back to Manno when I heard him start to squeal. He looked agitated and began shaking his head violently. The change in air pressure was crushing his eardrums, and his serene demeanor immediately vanished. He hammered at his ears with his palms and slammed his body into one side of the crate before rushing over to bodycheck the other side.

I wanted to open the crate to help him, but it would only have made matters worse. I tried to mime swallowing or yawning in the hopes that he might mimic me and equalize the pressure, but he was too upset and in too much discomfort to pay any attention to me.

When the plane finally rolled to a stop, I unbuckled my harness and hurried over to Manno with a bag of sunflower seeds. I filled my hands and stuck the seeds through the bars for him. I tried to coax him into eating even a little bit, but he was in no mood to eat.

I was anxious to make sure Manno was okay before he left my sight—I knew we weren't going to have much time together that night. We touched down at Al Maktoum International, a small airport about an hour outside of Dubai, but we would be departing the next day on a passenger flight from Dubai International. I was booked into a hotel near the airport, but this time, Manno wouldn't be staying with me. He had received royal treatment at the Rotana the night before, but tonight, he was just another parcel.

"Can I go with him to Dubai International?" I asked the ground crew as they began to undo the restraints on Manno's crate.

"No," a crew member said flatly. I tried to argue, but my pleas fell on deaf ears.

"It won't be long," I promised Manno as the ground crew wheeled him away. "Just one more day and you'll be there."

My skin prickled with nervousness as I watched Manno roll away from me. I wanted him to know that he was safe, but I was worried something would happen to him while he was out of my sight. What if his crate got lost in the sea of cargo, or worse, someone bribed the warehouse and Manno disappeared?

I barely slept that night. The next morning, after only a few hours' rest, I left my hotel and took a cab to the Dubai airport. There, I went to the first Emirates kiosk I saw and talked to a woman wearing the airline's uniform: a beige-colored skirt suit and red cabin-crew hat, with a white scarf draping down one side of her face.

"Excuse me," I said, "but I have an animal departing as cargo today and I need to check up on him."

Manno and I would be on a regular passenger plane this time, and I wouldn't be able to visit him once he was moved to the cargo compartment. I tried to imagine what Manno might be thinking and whether he was scared. I wanted to comfort him and have him see a familiar face before we left, so that he would know he wasn't alone.

"I'm sorry, I can only help with regular flights," she said. She referred me to an office on the other side of the terminal.

When I got to the office, there was only one Emirates staffer working, and a few people were already waiting in chairs. I took a number and joined them, hoping it wouldn't take more than a couple of minutes. When ten minutes passed and nothing happened, I began to get impatient. Finally, she called my number and I jumped to my feet.

"I have a chimpanzee en route to Kenya today."

"A chimpanzee?" she asked, somewhat startled. "You can't just check in exotic animals—they have to go through cargo."

I smiled. "I know. He's already in cargo. I'm trying to find him so I can check up on him."

"Then it's too late," she said. "You won't be able to see him until landing."

"What do you mean?"

"It is impossible."

"Could you tell me where he would be held if I *could* see him?"

"Cargo City," she said, "but—"

It was too late. I was already gone, sprinting outside the airport to the first cab I found.

"Take me to Cargo City, please," I said to the driver. A few minutes later, I stared out the window of the car and realized that Cargo City

was more than just a name. It was a district made up of three- and four-story square buildings, transport trucks crossing between them at every turn, and a jumble of modular steel trailers and refinery equipment waiting in the open. *Manno's in there somewhere*, I thought.

I spotted a building with an Emirates sign. "Stop right there," I blurted. The driver pulled over, shooting an annoyed look at me for hiring him for such a short fare.

I headed inside the Emirates building and asked the woman inside where the animals were. She gave me decent directions, but as soon as I stepped outside, I was overwhelmed by the noise and sheer size of the place. I stopped the first person in a blue smock that I saw.

"There's a chimpanzee here—I want to see it before we go," I told the worker.

The man cupped his ear.

"Sorry," he said, followed by a stream of Arabic.

I thanked him and hurried through the first building doors I reached. Once again, I went straight toward the first person in a uniform I saw.

"Excuse me," I said, jogging toward him. "Where would a chimpanzee be held?"

He pointed at a rectangular building that looked like all the others. I pointed to it, making sure we were talking about the same one, then hustled away, waving and shouting my thanks.

The front door opened to a small office operated by a man behind a front desk.

"I'm looking for an ape," I said to the worker.

He shook his head, no. I sighed and hurried back outside. My body was beading with perspiration in the dry Arab heat. I continued scurrying from one building to another asking for a chimpanzee, but between the dizzying inventory of crates and pallets and the language barrier, I was getting nowhere. I checked the time on my phone. It was 12:30 p.m., which meant I had thirty minutes to get to airport security or else I wasn't going anywhere.

I decided to try one more worker. "Do you know if a chimpanzee is around here?"

"*Champagne?*" he asked.

"No," I stuttered. "Ape?"

"Ah, animal," he said. "They will not let you see the animals."

"Okay, but can you take me there anyway?" He hesitated, but I gave him a look that said I wasn't taking no for an answer. "*Please?*"

After a pause, he said, "Follow me." I did—moving as slowly as I could to match his pace, frustrating as it was. After fifty meters, he pointed at a pair of swinging doors. I thanked him, then burst through the doors to the facility.

The room was air-conditioned halfway to becoming a refrigerator and illuminated with super-fluorescent bulbs. I clutched my body and blinked rapidly to acclimatize. There was a slightly battered wood desk but no one manning it. *Ding ding ding*—I pumped the call bell. A young man arrived from a small parcel area in the back.

"Excuse me," I said through deep breaths. "Do you speak English?"

"Of course," he replied with barely an accent.

"Is this where the live animals are?"

"In the back, yes," he said. "Is everything okay, sir?"

"I'm here to see my chimpanzee."

"Chimpanzee?" He furrowed his brow. "I'm sorry, sir, but the chimpanzee left five days ago."

I blinked in disbelief. I could have sworn the bulbs were glowing brighter. "Me and my chimpanzee arrived last night. From Erbil. I was with him."

"No, sir. There has to be a mistake."

Am I being lied to? Did someone—one of Ramadan's dealers perhaps—scoop up Manno in a last-ditch effort to get him back? The room was spinning.

He sensed my unease. "Let me search the area," he said.

Just then, another worker stepped out of the parcel room in a blue smock. "Are you talking about the monkey?"

"Yes!" I said. "The ape."

He reached under the desk and plopped a yellow lanyard on the desk. "You'll have to wear this." I did as instructed and followed him through a large warehouse, past pallets of packaged cargo. I entered the warehouse and immediately felt a pang of homesickness when I spotted a red Alaskan malamute. I resisted petting it. *Stick to the plan,* I thought to myself.

Finally, amongst the dog kennels, I spotted Manno's white crate. The logos for Animals Lebanon and Ol Pejeta jumped out at me, a much-needed dose of familiarity. I opened the slider on the top of the crate to look inside. Manno was curled up, his arms wrapped around his legs, as far back as he could be from the bars. I breathed a sigh of relief.

Manno groggily lifted his head from his slouch and saw me. His shredded paper was packed down. He didn't respond to my tickling, so I stroked his hand to reassure him he'd be safe. Looking into his tired brown eyes, I saw the face of every other mysterious chimpanzee that he was mistaken for. How many apes passed through this cargo area? And what were their destinations? Likely not the same as Manno's.

"Don't worry, little buddy," I said, trying to soothe Manno with my tone. "We're going to get you home."

Chapter twelve

"*The only thing necessary for the triumph of evil is for good people to do nothing.*"

—EDMUND BURKE

There are many things that Africa does well. Hospitality, music, charity. It's a long list. In my experience, however, bureaucracy is not one of them.

I was reminded of that while I stood in a crowd on the main level of Jomo Kenyatta International Airport in Nairobi, waiting to get a visa to stay in the country for a few days while Manno got settled at Sweetwaters. The queue kept getting longer, as men in suits walked to the front of the line with their families. I was eager to get through as quickly possible. Because I was such a last-minute addition to this part of the trip, I was worried that, if I took too long in customs, our contacts in Kenya would see me as an afterthought and transport Manno to Sweetwaters without me, leaving me stranded in Nairobi.

I finally reached the passport control desk, but they wouldn't allow me to pay for my visa with a credit card. *You should have known better*, I told myself, and withdrew Kenyan shillings from a bank machine. I asked an airport employee how much the US$50 visa fee was in Kenyan shillings and withdrew that amount, then returned to the front of the line, only to learn that it still wasn't enough.

By the time I got my visa, close to an hour had been wasted, and I

wasn't sure if Manno was even still in the airport. "If your monkey is still here, you will find him in cargo," the customs agent said, handing back my passport.

"He's an ape," I corrected the officer, already having become something of a primate snob.

I ran outside with my luggage and scanned the arrivals area. I was supposed to meet someone from the Project to End Great Ape Slavery (PEGAS). Seeing nobody holding a sign with my name, I hurried toward a throng of taxis instead, ducking past the scrum of African drivers trying to hustle me a ride and heading straight to the first car I saw with someone in the driver's seat. I opened the front passenger door and slid in. "Take me to cargo, please," I said, the stress apparent in my voice.

"Okay, no problem," the driver, a young Kenyan in a purple golf shirt, said cheerfully. He pulled out of the taxi lane and I slowed my breathing, telling myself to relax now that I was finally heading toward Manno. After a minute, the driver looked at me and said, "Where is cargo?"

"You're asking me?" I cursed under my breath in disbelief and shook my head. Sweat beaded on my forehead and I felt the mounting frustration in my chest. We were close to exiting the airport when I saw a mob of video cameras gathered behind an army green truck. Peering harder through the crowd, I caught a glimpse of the crate they were gathering around.

"There!" I shouted, pointing at the throng of people.

I paid the driver and hurried to the security checkpoint, where I exchanged my passport for a lanyard, which took far longer than I wanted it to. Finally, I was able to rush over and join the crowd.

I recognized my contact from PEGAS, Daniel Stiles, in the middle of the throng of people and pushed my way over to him.

"Daniel, we did it!" I exclaimed, clapping him on the back.

Daniel was with a handsome guy in his thirties, with hair buzzed to the scalp. He was wearing a green shirt with Ol Pejeta's logo stitched

on the chest, and he seemed to be supervising a couple of other men in similar uniforms.

"This is Dr. Stephen Ngulu," Daniel said, introducing me to one of the men. Stephen and I shook hands. "He is Ol Pejeta's lead vet and one of the top Kenya Wildlife Service veterinarians."

A couple of other Ol Pejeta staff hoisted Manno's crate onto the truck bed under a canvas canopy, while several video- and photojournalists shot from low angles. I dropped my bag and began shouldering my way through the scrum toward the truck. I could tell from the scratching pens and the bursts of camera clicks around me that Manno's arrival was bigger than I could have imagined.

I turned my attention to Manno's crate in the back of a canvas-covered truck. When I was just a few steps away, though, the truck suddenly started moving. I sprinted toward it and started running alongside his crate. I grazed a shrub with three-inch thorns that cut my arm, but I wiped away the blood and kept running until I was able to grab onto the back of the truck and climb over the tailgate, like a bandit hopping onto a moving train.

Once I was in, I lay still for a second to catch my breath. When I sat up, I noticed I was sharing the space with not only Manno's crate, but also a reporter, who gave me an odd look. I nodded politely, but then I heard rattling from inside Manno's crate. He was pulling at the bars, trying to escape. I fished the key from my pocket, unlocked the crate, and pulled the slider up. I reached my hands inside for him to hold.

"It's okay, little guy," I reassured him. "You're just about there. Just a couple more hours. You made it."

As soon as we exited the airport grounds, the convoy abruptly stopped and pulled over. Stephen and another Kenya Wildlife Services (KWS) veterinarian, Dr. Edward Kariuki, got out of the truck and came around to the back of the vehicle.

"Who has the crate key?" Stephen asked.

"I do," I said. I closed the slider on Manno's crate and snapped the padlock closed.

Stephen held out his hand for the key. For a moment, I thought about holding on to it—I was worried that if I handed it over, I'd be giving up the only thing that would allow me to see Manno's journey through to the end. But I knew I had to trust the experts. I handed the key to Stephen, who went over to the crate with a bundle of thick cord in his hand. He secured Manno's crate in place, and then got back into the cab of the canvas truck.

I went over to his window. "Can I get in with you guys?" I asked.

"There's no room in here," Stephen said from his seat between the driver and Edward. Stephen motioned with his chin to the station wagon ahead of them, where Daniel was squeezed in with four other passengers. They popped open the door for me and I squished in beside them. Thus began the four-hour journey to Sweetwaters, over rough terrain. *I hope Manno is more comfortable than this*, I thought.

It was night by the time we passed under the thatched roof of the entrance gate to Ol Pejeta, a 90,000-acre camp in the African savanna. The car's headlights illuminated the occasional zebra, but otherwise it was too dark on the unlit dirt road to make out the details of the conservancy. As we rambled closer to the 250-acre ape sanctuary known as Sweetwaters, Daniel gave me the lay of the land.

"They've essentially created two families of rescued chimps," he said. "One with two dozen members and the other with fourteen. That's the one they hope Manno will join."

"Why two families?" I asked. "Why not one?"

"So they don't kill each other," said Daniel matter-of-factly. "The families may be artificial, but they will war just as they would in their Central and West African native lands. Some naturalists don't like this . . . 'social engineering,' they call it. Well, maybe fifty years ago, when there were three and a half million chimps, I'd agree. But there are only a quarter million left on Earth. We can't afford to lose another, no matter how natural the means of death."

"Has that ever happened here?" I asked.

"One chimp was killed by a snake bite," Daniel said. "And we had

a bad introduction once. We introduced a male, thinking the family would accept him. They did, at first, but then . . ." He just shook his head.

We arrived at an area called the Stables, a long rectangular building and surrounding huts. It wasn't far from Ol Pejeta's utilitarian offices, which were reserved for visiting researchers and their staff, filmmakers, security trainers, and the like. The truck with Manno was forty minutes or so behind us, moving slower to protect Manno on the winding and bumpy roads.

"I'm going to get something to eat," Daniel said. "Are you hungry?"

"No thanks," I said. "I'll wait for Manno."

He shrugged, like *fair enough*. I waited until Daniel was inside and then wandered onto the dark, dirt road, marching toward a fork in the road that the truck would have to pass after the gate. I waited in the pitch black for thirty minutes or so, seeing little around me in the light of the moon and listening to the wildness of Africa, until small white lights and the sound of an engine finally approached from the distance. As the first vehicle came to a stop in front of me, I saw it was manned by two Kenyan soldiers.

"Do you know where the doctors are with the new chimp?" I asked.

They pointed behind to another pair of headlights approaching, the familiar canvas-covered back coming into view. As the second vehicle pulled up, I stepped in front of it, raising my hand until it came to a stop.

"Hey," I said, approaching the driver's side of the vehicle. I spoke to Stephen, sitting beside the driver. "Can you take me along to wherever you're taking Manno?"

"No," said Stephen, his voice deep and thick.

"What!?" I exclaimed. "Why not?"

"The chimpanzee has been declared quarantined."

"Since when?"

"Since the airport."

"For how long?"

"Four months."

I shook my head and asked him to repeat it. "Look," I said, "I've been with Manno for the last two days, it's fine. Just start the quarantine tomorrow."

"Please step out of the way," Edward, the other vet, said flatly.

I didn't want to move. "I just traveled with Manno from a war zone to bring him to this sanctuary—I've been working to get him here for three years. At least let me go with you to say goodbye."

Stephen, betraying a bit of agitation, shook his head. "It's not going to happen."

"This animal wouldn't be here if it weren't for me," I barked. I knew full well that there were many more people involved in his rescue, but I was desperate.

"And if it were not for us, he would not even be allowed in Kenya," Stephen shot back. "It is us that allowed him in, and it is us who must comply with protocol to ensure the safety of Kenya's people to be protected from disease."

"Listen—"

"No!" he snapped. "You listen! It is my license on the line." The whites of his eyes glistened in the moonlight. "If the authorities find out his quarantine has been violated, they can euthanize him! Do you want that?"

That was the last thing I wanted, of course, but I was stubborn. "Fine. But I'm following you there."

He scoffed. "You are a crazy white man."

"Go! I'm right behind you." It had taken me three years. I wasn't about to quit now.

They looked at each other and called my bluff. "This is Africa," Stephen said. "You don't know anything about what is out there." They drove away.

I started walking down the dirt road, muttering to myself as I

followed the truck's taillights until they eventually dissolved into the darkness. There was obviously a disconnect between how we saw Manno. To the caretakers, he was an endangered animal; to me, Manno was a friend. He was about to spend 120 days in what amounted to solitary confinement. What about his psychological well-being? I wanted him to see a friendly face and feel reassured that he was safe now.

I kicked up dust from the dirt road, fuming. I thought the quarantine hut would be just around the corner, but I was now a couple hundred meters down the road, in the pitch-black darkness, and there was nothing in sight. It suddenly occurred to me that the electric fence that I was approaching must serve an important purpose—it divided the residencies from the game reserve. *What am I doing? I'm in the middle of the African savanna, amongst lions, buffalos, and a host of other deadly animals that I know absolutely nothing about.* I thought of Anders and remembered I was now a father. I couldn't afford to be so rash.

I turned back, walking as quickly and quietly as I could to the house, still hearing the roars just outside the gate, imagining myself ending up on the news and the viewers all saying, "Stupid crazy white guy got exactly what he deserved." I was relieved when I saw the light of the stables. As I walked in, I saw Daniel on his phone.

"Yes, he's right here," Daniel said. I knew it was Stephen checking up on me.

I made it to my Spartan room, pulled back the nylon mosquito net, and lay on my bed, unable to sleep. I struggled to accept that the last time I saw my friend, he was thrashing around in his crate, trying to escape, and looking at me with pained eyes. How could that be our goodbye?

Maybe it was rest I needed to wake up rejuvenated, or maybe it was my love of early mornings, the rust-colored sunrise over the acacia-covered plains clicking with cicadas and birds under the distant

shadow of Mount Kenya. Whatever it was, when I stepped outside the next morning, the surrounding African huts took me back a decade to my first trip to Africa, and I felt a twinge of the optimism I'd been filled with on my first trip.

Eight years ago, I had been a schoolteacher volunteering on my vacation, trying to do some good for people who lived on the margins of the world. And though my knowledge of their plights was limited and my ability to help them often constrained, I had learned that I could be a part of the solution, however small that part was. If it was a drop in the bucket, at least it was one drop of goodness more. That morning, I reminded myself to maintain that same optimism. That's what had gotten Manno here in the first place, after all.

I wandered to a covered outdoor patio where a few staff were having an English breakfast and tea. Stephen and Edward spotted me, and they each shot me a big smile. An apology was more than warranted, so I took my plate to their table.

"I'm so sorry for the way I acted last night," I said to them. "You didn't deserve that."

"It's fine, Spencer," Stephen said. "We know you meant well."

"We just have to be extra careful," said Edward.

"Why is that?" I asked, sitting down beside them.

"Manno is the first rescue Sweetwaters has had since the Ebola outbreak a few years ago," Stephen explained. "The government has issued very strict measures about which animals can be rescued from certain regions. This has to go perfectly if we want to rescue more animals. We must abide by their rules. If Manno were to be a carrier of the virus, they wouldn't send him back to Iraq—they would euthanize him."

I shuddered, imagining my little buddy being put to sleep and everyone's work over the past three years coming to nothing.

"And if they learn we did something wrong," Edward said, "they may never let us bring another ape here again." The thought of the many other trafficked apes whose futures I could have put at risk sent a shiver down my spine.

Stephen invited me out to the Sweetwaters sanctuary, not to see Manno, but to meet his future family. We slid into a Land Rover, and Stephen fired up the engine. We rumbled along the same dusty path Stephen had driven the previous night with Manno in the back. We passed through the livestock gate, attached to an electric fence meant to keep the more ferocious animals in the reserve away from the residence. We turned the corner, and immediately came to a stop—just a few meters from the gate, a pride of lions lounged under an acacia tree. A lioness, face crimson from her kill, was tearing apart the remains of a black-and-white striped carcass by the side of the road. My blood ran cold—to think I had even considered chasing after the truck in that wilderness. *Good thing I stopped when I did last night*, I thought. We maneuvered around the pride, and another fifteen minutes of road reinforced the realization that I'd never have made it back to the sanctuary if I'd gone out that far.

We finally came to a small enclosure, where Stephen parked the car. We walked along a dirt path beside a long wire fence that stretched around hundreds of acres of natural vegetation. "Would you like to meet Ol Pejeta's other star?" asked Stephen. I nodded, and we got back in the cream-colored truck and drove some distance until we arrived at a wooden gate.

"This is Sudan," Stephen said. He swung the gate open, and I saw the rhino, his wrinkled body caked with mud, listlessly grazing on the field. His cuplike ears twitched to shoo away flies that buzzed around the blunt horns on his head.

"Sudan is the last male [northern] white rhino left in the world," said Stephen. "Do you want to pet him?"

"Yes!" I said.

"Come on his right side where he can see you and know you mean no harm," Stephen instructed. "He's blind in the other eye." I caressed Sudan's stub of a horn, smooth to the touch, and ran my palms across his gray hide, which felt more like patting a thick leather jacket than a living animal. His 2,000-kilogram body felt unmovable, but he was actually quite feeble and critically ill. Sudan would die barely a year

later, officially marking the end of his species—a travesty that happened on our watch, perpetuated by humanity's carelessness, greed, and lack of urgent concern for our world and its inhabitants.

I patted Sudan's side one last time, utterly in awe of him, before following Stephen back to the gravel road. We passed through the visitors' area at the northwest enclosure and headed toward a two-story, dark brown building surrounded by a yard that was riddled with tires, cement blocks, and climbing poles. The area looked largely lifeless, save for a man in tan coveralls crouching over some pails. We walked through a wire gate into the enclosure and greeted the man as he sorted bananas and sliced guava and melons.

There was a heavy-duty steel door about four feet tall on the main level of the building. It dropped open with a clang. Hoots and shrieks echoed out of the hole, getting louder and louder until the chimps themselves poured out, one by one, hulking males and powerful females. They landed on their knuckles and immediately started chasing each other around the yard, wrestling and climbing, rolling over the cement blocks to simultaneously scratch their backs and bask in the sun. There were fourteen of them in all, socializing just as they would in the wild. It was a remarkable thing considering that each of the chimps we were looking at had, at one point, been an orphan. All of them had endured horrific things and unnatural isolation that left some with post-traumatic stress disorder. Having the company of other chimps was the closest thing to a cure.

The biggest male chimp sashayed with authority toward the feeder, the other chimps clearing the way for him. Each of his footsteps made a light thud on the ground as he came closer.

"This is Niyonkuru," Stephen said. "His name means 'God is the highest.' He was saved from an illegal vendor trying to sell him to conservationists in Burundi. When we received him, he was terribly depressed with scars on his thighs from the rope leashes they put on him. That was nineteen years ago. Today, he is the highest ranking member of the tribe."

Niyonkuru squatted inside the fence and deftly caught the banana tossed at him. He peeled the top open with his teeth and ate it in two bites.

"It is important that we feed him first to maintain the natural hierarchy," Stephen told me. "We start at the highest ranking, then move lower and lower, to avoid conflict. If anyone lower has a full belly before him, he will act with aggression." He pointed to a thick, younger male sitting behind Niyonkuru, intently watching him eat.

"This is William, their 'president-elect,'" Stephen explained. "He will eventually depose Niyonkuru—it's just a matter of time. When William came ten years ago, he was an outsider but since then he's won the respect of the whole pack, except for one." The keeper tossed a guava fruit to Niyonkuru and a banana to his successor, who tore it open with his teeth and pressed the banana into his mouth like a rod through a hole.

If Manno was to successfully integrate, he would have to find acceptance from William, Niyonkuru, and a third male, a goal made all the more difficult because of the contest between alpha males happening before our eyes.

But we were getting ahead of ourselves. First Manno had to make friends with all eight females, beginning with Akeela, one of the oldest and most motherly members of the tribe, though she was still formidable and intimidating in her own right. She'd arrived from a small cage in an apartment where she had been kept as a pet, and when she arrived, she displayed unusually bad coordination and balance. The vet thought the disorder was caused by neurological damage. But over time, Akeela healed and became an exceptionally doting mother to each of the baby chimps when they arrived.

Manno was not a baby anymore. He was older than William was when he'd arrived, and Manno knew nothing of chimpanzee social behavior. If he couldn't form a bond with Akeela—the foundation of the "Sisterhood Protection Society" that would save him from male aggressors—there was little hope for him at Sweetwaters.

Watching the alpha male chew his guava and melons and spit seeds at his feet, I was reminded of the 98 percent DNA we humans share with chimps. For Manno, who likely hadn't been touched by another chimp, let alone held by one, since the day his mother was killed four years ago, that bond was much stronger. He had been raised to believe he wasn't one of them, he was one of us. Over time, his bond with humans would hopefully lessen as Manno formed new relationships with his kind.

I was hopeful that one day Manno would walk across this yard with the others, and maybe, years from now, that he'd be squatting in Niyonkuru's footprints.

As I bounded down the escalator into the Edmonton airport's arrival terminal a few days later, my heart skipped a beat at the sound of Anders's tiny voice calling out at me. I scanned the crowd and saw him in Christie's arms, holding his favorite companion of the day: a toy excavation truck.

"Daddy!" he squealed. His body squirmed and legs kicked until Christie put him down. He dropped his truck and sprinted toward me, his little legs moving as fast as they could. I scooped him up in my arms, and when he wrapped his chubby little arms around my neck and buried his head into my shoulder, I felt happiness radiating through every fiber of my body.

I shifted him over to one arm and wrapped my other around Christie's shoulders, pulling her in for a kiss.

"How'd it go?" she asked, as we walked outside to the parking lot, Anders sitting on my hip the same way Manno used to do.

"I'd say about as well as we could have hoped," I said.

"We saw you on the news," said Christie.

"Yeah, the media attention helped to up the ante. We did all we could do. We gave him a chance. At least now, if nothing else, Manno has the opportunity to live a good life."

"You can't ask for more than that," Christie said.

We found our truck and I buckled Anders into his child seat. I handed him his toy to busy his hands while Christie drove the fifty-kilometer stretch home. Though there were so many questions about Manno's future still to be answered, I could not worry about that right now. After three days of stress, my reserves for worrying were drained, not to mention I was fatigued, as I was still on Eastern Africa Time. At the moment, I was just happy to be back with my family.

Christie pulled into the driveway, and before I even opened my door, I heard a warm and familiar Wookie voice barking at me.

Christie and I had told ourselves that we'd wait until Anders was five before getting another dog. We wanted him to be old enough to help us train the dog into a well-behaved pet. But then we met a young woman working two jobs who was struggling to give her young malamute-husky mix the necessary time and attention the breed required. And as soon as we met Tux, we knew he had to be a part of our family, and we were overjoyed when the woman graciously agreed to allow us to adopt him.

As soon as the garage door rose, Tux jumped on his hind legs and licked my free hand, howling joyfully. I scratched behind his pinned-down ears and across his sable fur coat, and smiled into his eyes.

Coming home always filled me with profound gratitude. Each time I returned to my loving family, to a peaceful home in the middle of a jack pine and spruce forest, to a tap of clean running water and a consistent source of electricity, to safe and orderly streets, I would wonder, *Why do I ever leave this place?* Perspective, of course. Without travel, I might get caught up in the littlest thing—a cutoff in traffic, a trivial squabble at work, the internet being a tad slow—but the broader world puts all that nonsense into perspective.

This homecoming felt different, though. The feeling of immense gratitude still pulsed through me as I turned from Christie to Tux to

Anders, but now as I looked into my son's bright blue eyes, I hoped that I was leaving a legacy for him. I'd figured out long ago how important it was to live a life worth living. Now I was trying to live by example, for him.

I wanted Anders to know that he could accomplish anything in this world as long as he had his heart in the right place, put his mind to it, didn't take no for an answer, and was humble enough to accept help along the way. I wanted him to know that his life was interconnected with billions more. With Melissa, the inspiring young woman who sent me forth on this journey years ago. With the countless wonderful students who I have been fortunate enough to teach and who have taught me far more than I could ever hope to teach them. With Francis, Mariatu, and their family, who changed my life. With Engineer Yousef and all the unbelievably wonderful owners who adopted the dogs he helped me rescue from Kabul. With Sulaiman, Jason, Maggie, Cheryl, Ramadan, and Abdulqadir and his family. With Manno.

More than anything else, I wanted Anders to know that maybe he didn't have to change the whole world. If saving Manno had taught me anything, it was that saving one world was more than enough.

Epilogue

"It's impossible," said Pride.
"It's risky," said Experience.
"It's pointless," said Reason.
"Give it a try," said the Heart.

—UNKNOWN

The caretakers counted to three and lifted the crate off the concrete and carefully transported it from inside the quarantine shack to the back of a miniature yellow truck.

It was March 31, 2017—just four months after I had last seen Manno through the slider of his crate. Richard Vigne, the executive director of Ol Pejeta, had emailed me to say Manno was ready to begin his integration after a successful quarantine. He invited me to come for the event, warning me that I wouldn't be able to hold Manno, though we could interact through the bars of his enclosure. With Christie's blessing, once again, I was on the next flight to Nairobi.

I stood on the sidelines with Vigne, Stephen Ngulu, Daniel Stiles, Edward Kariuki, Alicia Melis—a primatologist doing research at Sweetwaters—and a number of the organization's staff, all of us privileged and pleased to witness this moment. As we gathered, a family of four elephants wandered out of the wilderness inside the enclosure, as though we were in a Disney movie and they were welcoming Manno to his new home.

I turned to Stephen and Edward. "I just want to apologize one more time for that first night," I said, shaking my head.

"We were wondering, 'Who is this crazy *mzungu*?'" said Stephen as the two of them chuckled.

After Manno's crate was securely in place, the two doctors jumped in the front of the truck and drove toward the main enclosure, while the rest of us followed in another Land Rover. As the elephants trumpeted at the bright blue sky, I couldn't help but smile at the perfection of it all.

Of course, this wasn't the end just yet. Manno was merely being moved to the chimp house at Sweetwaters Chimpanzee Sanctuary for an integration process that could last up to three times longer than his quarantine, and success wasn't guaranteed.

I recognized the dark brown building that Stephen had shown me on my first trip. Manno's soon-to-be family was spread throughout the outdoor sanctuary. William was no longer "president-elect"; he was firmly in charge now. He swung maniacally from branch to branch—clearly exhibiting "display," the chimp version of driving a Ferrari with the speakers blasting. I looked for Niyonkuru but couldn't make him out in the pack. He was now just another male.

The convoy came to a stop and everyone applauded. The caretakers unloaded the crate from the truck and shuffled it sideways into the building, carrying Manno into the central corridor.

The main floor of the building was separated into two halves and three empty enclosures. Each room had white corner walls between the steel bars and was furnished with shelves, piles of hay, tire swings, hammocks, and vegetation. There were two adjacent rooms to the left of us, and a larger one to our right that connected to the yard.

"These are the dormitories," Stephen explained. "The chimpanzees sleep at night here, allowing us to check on them every evening."

"Check for what?" I asked.

"Make sure they're happy and healthy."

"And that they are all still here," added Edward.

Stephen unlocked the caged door to the center enclosure and held

it open for us. He opened the second enclosure door, but only the caretakers were allowed to enter. They set the crate down on the floor and slid the front door open. From here on, the goal was to minimize Manno's human contact, lest he still think he was one of us.

My old friend was curled up in the corner of his crate, slowly breathing as he stared through the opening into the bright room. The caretakers called his name and Manno reared his head before tumbling out of the crate. He somersaulted around the room, swinging from the hammocks and ropes, hooting and panting, happy as could be.

I pressed up against the cage and stuck my arms through the bars. "Manno, Manno," I said. When he didn't turn back, I wondered if he'd forgotten me again. I wasn't hurt by it this time, as his integration was so much bigger than our friendship. But when he did finally look at me—and flung himself in my direction—my heart fluttered. He leapt at me from a shelf and gripped the bars with outstretched limbs, splayed like a starfish, and laughed as I tickled his belly.

After he picked at my scalp for a few seconds, Manno's attention turned suddenly to the sight over my shoulder, across the entire building and through the open door to the yard. Before arriving at Sweetwaters, Manno likely hadn't seen another chimp since the day he and his brother were sold to separate Iraqi zoos. He probably didn't remember what they looked or sounded like—let alone what it was like to live amongst a family of them. The high-pitched screams echoing from their jungle enclosure outside and the sight of fourteen adult chimps chasing each other around the yard was foreign to him, and the look on his suddenly silent face was nothing short of primal fear.

It only got worse from there. Later that day, Akeela, the female chimp chosen to be Manno's surrogate mother, was brought into the adjacent enclosure, keeping a safe distance between them in order to prevent Manno from being overwhelmed by her—or worse.

Akeela was chosen for her tender nature with younger chimps— she was a consummate mother who'd adopted chimps even older

than Manno before. Though she didn't exhibit any aggression—and showed lots of interest in Manno—he wouldn't even make eye contact with her or come within touching distance of her. When the rest of the family returned to the dormitories for the night, he crumpled into a fetal position, completely overwhelmed.

By the third day, we were quite concerned.

"He's not doing well, psychologically speaking," Alicia, the researcher, said as I stood with Stephen and Richard outside his enclosure. Manno huddled on a high shelf on the other side of the room, placing himself as far away as he could be from the other chimps, the only place it seemed he felt safe.

"He has to learn that he's a chimp," said Stephen.

"He might adapt better if he's relaxed," Alicia said. "I think it might be of some benefit to him to have a familiar face. Someone to transition him. Spencer?"

I knew that, at some point, getting into Manno's enclosure would be a threat to my life—and when that day came, it would show that Manno had successfully integrated. But at that point, Manno was just a soft-hearted, scared little boy who needed the comfort of an old friend.

"Put me in," I said.

The heavy metal door latch clacked and the hinges creaked open. I entered, and Stephen closed the door behind me. Manno was on a shelf near the ceiling, his back turned to me. I softly called his name, "Manno." He looked down and immediately leapt across the enclosure onto a lower shelf next to where I was standing and, without hesitation, fell into my arms. As I felt his coarse hair rubbing under my chin and the warmth of his little breaths on my neck, it seemed as though no time had passed at all.

I whispered into his ear, "I love you, buddy." I held him quietly for a moment, cherishing the moment, not sure when—or if—I'd experience it again.

I hoped to bask in this magical moment a little longer, but

Manno's attention quickly went elsewhere. He hopped back onto a shelf and stretched out his gangly arms. After a few soft tickles, I scratched all over his body. Then I sat down on the floor with him and stroked his face. It felt so good to see him relax. The hour went by in an instant, and when it was time for me to go, Stephen had to pry Manno off me.

It was the last time I'd ever hold Manno. The next day, it was time for me to go home again, and it wasn't clear when I'd be able to return.

Over the following weeks, Stephen and the other chimpanzee caretakers continued their efforts to get Akeela to adopt Manno, but no matter how hard she tried, Manno wouldn't let her get close to him. She made countless efforts—making gestures of benevolence and kindness with outstretched arms and legs—but Manno wouldn't come closer than a meter and, more often than not, ran in the opposite direction of her.

After a month and a half of failed efforts, the caretakers tried a different tactic. Akeela was removed, and Jane, a chimp closer to Manno's age who had been adopted by Akeela, was brought in. The caretakers hoped that Manno would allow the teenage chimp to care for him the way Akeela often tried to care for baby bucks and warthogs she captured from the bush.

Instead of showing a motherly instinct toward Manno, though, Jane exhibited more of a playful, sisterly side. She clapped and blew raspberries at him through the barrier, trying to get him to play with her. At times Manno would approach her, but he still wouldn't let her touch him.

Sometimes, though, he'd crawl close enough to the bars for Jane to graze him. One day, he got close enough for her to hold his feet, and he didn't scurry away. It was the first time he'd felt the warm touch of another chimpanzee since being snatched from his mother's arms four years ago.

When they were finally put in the same enclosure, Jane climbed

over Manno's legs and wrapped her arms around him. She tickled him and Manno began to laugh. In a matter of days, Manno and Jane were sleeping in the same space together, inseparable siblings.

One by one, the staff introduced the other females to Manno, beginning with Bahati, who joined Jane in cuddling Manno, and then Akeela again, followed by Tess, Joy, Chipie, Dufa, and Amisero. They all wanted to play with Manno. No matter how standoffish he acted initially, he eventually relented, accepted their grooming, and bonded with them all.

Finally, it was time to introduce Manno to the other males in the vast natural enclosure, a process that could still go horribly wrong if he was perceived as a threat to the hierarchy.

They began with the former alpha male, Niyonkuru, bringing him to Manno's enclosure while the females were inside with him. Things got off to a bad start, through no fault of Niyonkuru's or Manno's. It was the females—they saw Niyonkuru as a danger to their new little brother. Dufa, especially, was overprotective of Manno, biting Niyonkuru's fingers through the bars when he tried to touch her friend.

The females eventually warmed up to having Niyonkuru around Manno, and when the two males were finally in the same enclosure, Niyonkuru proved he was simply looking for a playmate after all. The next male, Roy, quickly took to Manno, as did Romeo and Uruhara, both of whom chased Manno around gleefully. There were only two chimps left to meet: Kisa and William, the alpha male expected to jealously protect the status he only recently earned.

The day he was set to meet William, Manno was released into the big outdoor enclosure with the whole family. He was overjoyed to be in the yard, quickly taking to the trees and wooden tower, but he had no idea he was sharing it with the fiercest chimp in the troop. As Joy groomed Manno in a tunnel to escape the heat, William saw his opportunity to put the interloper in his place.

William stomped toward Manno, grunting and huffing. Joy spotted him and shrieked a distinct alert to the sisterhood, and all of the

females hurried to Manno's defense. The female chimps formed a blockade between William and Manno and attacked the alpha male when he tried to get through them. They wouldn't let him put a finger on their little brother.

That was the moment we knew he'd made it. After six months, Manno's integration was deemed a success. Manno was a chimpanzee again.

Not long after Manno was accepted into the group, I received an image that I came to cherish. In it, Manno is riding on Jane's back with his arms wrapped around her chest, head on her shoulders. It's a sight you might see of a mother chimp carrying her toddler around in the wild. The day I saw it, I couldn't wait to show it to my students.

After a yearlong sabbatical from teaching, I was back in the classroom teaching to a new batch of teenagers who were only beginning to understand themselves, their world, and their purpose in it.

I told them the story of how I became a traveler in my midforties, the perspectives that people on other continents had given me, and the gratitude I'd gained along the way. I told them how cultivating curiosity for the outside world could lead them to chance encounters that just might make the world a better place than how they'd found it, so long as they kept their hearts and minds open.

I told them the story of Manno and then I projected that photo of Manno and Jane. "I know that we didn't change the world," I said, "but we changed his world."

"So, like, is Manno putting Jane in the friend zone?" asked a boy with an adolescent attempt at humor.

"It's more of a brother-sister kind of thing," I said, with a laugh.

"I think it's sweet," said one girl, a little teary-eyed.

I turned off the projector and sat at the edge of my desk. "If there's one thing I want you to take from this, it's this: Live your dreams. We only have one shot at this. Your life is a blank slate," I said. "Through determination and trying to be a good person, and the unwavering support of a beautiful partner, I've been lucky enough to have a lot

of really incredible once-in-a-lifetime experiences. The people I have met along the way and the relationships that we developed only added meaning and depth to these events. Your life is an empty page waiting to be written, an untouched canvas, so go paint your masterpiece with a palette of kindness."

Acknowledgments

There are so many people to thank, but I'd like to start with my wingman, Omar Mouallem. You did the heavy lifting of this project, buddy. You are a true artist. This book has been a lot of fun. Thank you for telling my story in such a beautiful way.

Brendan May, my editor extraordinaire, thank you for keeping me on track and keeping my eyes on the prize.

To Andrea Huncar, Tim Sawa, and Bob McKeown of the CBC, thanks for bringing attention to this story.

My agents, Rachel and Brian Wood. Rachel, thank you for guiding me over the past fifteen years, making this happen, and taking the time to read that piece oh so long ago.

Kyla Sentes, the spirit of your work is reflected throughout this book.

Jane Goodall, Nechirvan Barzani, and Cheryl Bernard: through your connections and help, all this was able to happen. Thank you for everything.

To the staff at Sweetwaters, thank you for taking care of my friend Manno as well as all of the other chimpanzees that truly need you.

Jason Mier, none of this would have been possible without you,

my friend. Your patience and calmness, even in a time of turmoil, was an example to behold.

Mom and Dad, thank you for teaching me to respect the planet and for showing me the value of hard work.

To all of my numerous students, friends, and colleagues, thank you all for listening and offering me advice and support throughout this entire process.

Chloe, Mac, Keena, and Tux, thank you for opening my heart to the love only an animal can awaken and for introducing me to the love of my life.

Anders, this story began before you came along, and you inspired me to see it through. As you get older, I hope that this story can be a reminder for you and your children to protect our planet and all its inhabitants. Anything is possible with the help of other good people and dogged determination. You inspire me to lead by example, my son.

And thanks most of all to Christie. I love you for allowing me to take on these risks and for supporting me throughout. You have made me a better person in every way, and your steadfast encouragement on this journey has led me to places I only imagined could exist. I would not have been able to follow my dreams without your support, encouragement, and inspiration. You've always believed in me, even when I doubted myself. Thank you.